Some of the
WAYS of GOD in HEALING

Some of the
WAYS
of
GOD
in
HEALING

Joy Dawson

YWAM Publishing
A Ministry of Youth With A Mission
Seattle, Washington 98155

Some of the Ways of God in Healing

Copyright © 1991 by Joy Dawson

Published by YWAM Publishing, a division of Youth With A Mission; P. O. Box 55787, Seattle, WA 98155

All Scriptures are from the New International Version of the Bible unless stated in the text.

ISBN 0-92754-514-4

Printed in the United States of America

Dedication

To my precious life partner, Jim, whose
faithful and loving support over forty-three
years has greatly helped to make this book
a reality.

With deep gratitude....

To God for His enabling grace to write this book in the midst of a heavy schedule, including much travel, message preparation, and teaching, along with loads of correspondence and very limited secretarial help.

To intercessor friends who pray regularly for me.

To my best friend and husband Jim, for his continuous willingness to listen and comment constructively.

To my dear part-time secretary, Janet Lambert, for her major contribution in typing the manuscript.

To Janet Benge for her helpful editorial suggestions.

Table of Contents

Foreword

As a boy of twelve, I remember sitting on the front pew wide-eyed as they carried in a woman who seemed more dead than alive. Members of her family carefully laid her skeleton-like frame on a cot which had been placed at the front of the church. In hushed tones, the congregation was told that this lady was riddled with cancer. The doctors had predicted she had only hours to live.

I stared at the woman, almost holding my breath. My dad and a visiting minister made their way to the woman lying on her cot. Together, they placed their hands upon her forehead and prayed. What happened next will never leave me. In fact, if I had not kept my eyes glued on the woman in those fateful moments, I would have suspected that the wasted one was somehow replaced by another healthy woman. She sprang to her feet! Then as the congregation went wild, she began to run, fast, around the auditorium, shouting, *"I'm healed! I'm healed!"*

It was simple, powerful, and undeniable. Why isn't it always like that? Later in life I watched, grieved, as an evangelist castigated a man in a wheelchair because he hadn't summoned enough faith to be healed. I also remember the irony of still another occasion: a very sincere brother looked at me through strong prescription glasses, flashing a smile reinforced with silver fillings, and told me that I, too, could have perfect, divine health like his if I would accept his theological view of healing.

That is why I am so grateful for this book by Joy Dawson. It is balanced, scriptural, and life-giving. It will answer many questions and pave the way for people to not only receive healing, but to more fully understand the ways of God.

During the 24 years I have known Joy, I have seen her teaching bring freedom and healing to multitudes around the world. I have also watched her weep with compassion as she prayed for dying refugee babies in Thailand. Often I have seen her counsel and pray with someone into the early hours of the morning, even though she had just spent a long, arduous day in ministry. I, too, have experienced God's healing power as she and her husband Jim ministered to me. I also know something of the many hours she spends with God, seeking Him and interceding for others. The Bible says: *"By their fruits you shall know them."* (Matthew 7:20 NKJV)

I recommend this book to you. I also commend to you the life, character, and wisdom of the author. She truly is one who practices what she teaches and teaches what the Bible says.

Loren D. Cunningham
Founder & President
Youth With A Mission

Preface

I want to make it very clear from the outset that I do not think I have all the answers in relation to this subject. That is why the title is *Some of the Ways of God in Healing*.

I want to make it equally clear that I have not attempted to present a complete study of this vast subject from God's Word. It is simply an honest attempt to put into writing some of the Biblical principles I have discovered and applied in personal experience related to this subject. It also contains some of my observations of the fascinating diversity of God's ways with His children as they pursue the knowledge of Him in order to make Him known.

God's intention is that we become more like His beloved Son, the Lord Jesus. And He causes, allows and uses many different and difficult circumstances to bring about that transformation.

Sickness and healing whether instantaneous, gradual, delayed, partial, through scientific medical means or without, or no healing at all, are all a part of that process.

I have shared a number of stories in this book how God has taught me His ways through times of physical pain. These experiences have been spread over a lifetime. I do not want to imply that I have suffered much through illness. On the contrary, God has mercifully granted me remarkable health.

It is my earnest desire and fervent prayer that from reading this book, many will come to a greater understanding of God's character and the principles by which He operates in the affairs of mankind.

Section One

Conditions
Keys
Causes

1

An Open-minded Approach to the Word of God

Have you struggled with questions related to healing? If so, you are not alone; most thinking Christians have.

Why are some healed and others not? Particularly when those who are not, are sometimes the most devout and sincere Christians.

I wonder what Trophimus thought when Paul had to leave him behind in Miletus because he was sick (II Timothy 4:20)?

Why do some of the most godly, vital Christians die while many who cause a lot of problems live on?

I wonder what the disciples thought when John the Baptist was beheaded (Matthew 14:10-12)?

Is God capricious? Does He have favorites? Is He really just in *all* His ways?

I wonder what the *other* mothers in the town of Nain thought when their dead sons *weren't* raised to life by Jesus during that time (Luke 7:11-15)?

Some of the Ways of God in Healing

What part does God play in relation to sickness? Does He have purposes for it?

I wonder if the Apostle Paul had questions when he had a severe eye disorder at the time of ministering to the Galatian Christians (Galatians 4:13-15)—after being used so mightily to bring God's healing power to others (Acts 19:11-12)?

What part, if any, do satanic forces play in relation to sickness?

What part do we play?

What part does medical science play?

Did "doctor" Luke have a conflict in combining his medical knowledge and experience with the miraculous healings he saw in his lifetime?

The more we honestly study this subject from God's Word, the more we realize there is no simple formula or single verse that explains it all.

As so often is the case with God's truths, we discover that while they are not complicated, there is a lot to learn.

However, God's Word is wonderfully balanced, simply because God is the author. *"All scripture is God-breathed and is useful for teaching, rebuking, correcting and training in righteousness, so that the man of God may be thoroughly equipped for every good work"* (II Timothy 3:16-17).

God's Word is intriguing, compelling, absorbing and full of wonder; as fresh and as dependable as tomorrow morning's sunrise; just like God Himself.

So let us attempt to take an unbiased look at this fascinating subject of sickness and healing from God's love letter to us...the Bible. He hasn't left us

An Open-minded Approach to the Word of God

without answers, although at times we may feel confused.

To all who will honestly pray, "Show me Your ways," He will repay with understanding. Jesus took a group of disillusioned, disappointed, discouraged disciples and sovereignly *"...opened their minds so they could understand the Scriptures"* (Luke 24:45).

Whether or not we identify with the disciples at that time in their lives, God wants to give us the same experience. No one has all the truth, except the One who is the truth—Jesus (John 14:6).

We're all pilgrims walking along a narrow road, discovering more about Him.

I was impressed with the genuine humility of a senior Baptist minister, when he announced soon after he took over the pastorate of a church I attended, that he knew he didn't have a handle on all the truth. He then quoted the final stanza of a hymn: "There is yet more light and truth to break forth from His Word."

To me this was refreshingly different from so many preachers and teachers who had strongly conveyed they had all the light.

When I came to write this book, I remembered again how I was gripped with that stanza. So I wrote to a secretary of the church I had attended many years ago in New Zealand to see if she could find the name of the hymn writer so I could give the appropriate acknowledgement.

To my surprised delight, she sent me the following three verses, having tracked down the hymn from an old Baptist hymnal. George Rawson, the author, has captured in a most poignant way exactly what I want to convey at this point. Each time I read it through, my heart is thrilled and stirred. Don't miss a line!

"We limit not the truth of God,
To our poor reach of mind,
By notions of our day and sect,
Crude, partial and confined;
No, let a new and better hope
Within our hearts be stirred:
The Lord has yet more light and truth
To break forth from His Word.

"Who dares to bind to his dull sense
The oracles of heaven,
For all the nations, tongues and climes,
And all the ages given?
That universe, how much unknown!
That ocean unexplored!
The Lord has yet more light and truth
To break forth from His Word.

"O Father, Son and Spirit, send
Us increase from above;
Enlarge, expand all Christian souls
To comprehend Thy love:
And make us to go on to know,
With nobler powers conferred,
The Lord has yet more light and truth
To break forth from His Word."

Let's make the last verse a personal prayer before we look into His Word.

2

Promises and Conditions

I'm absolutely convinced from the Word of God that divine healing is a part of God's overall plan for His children today, and that God intends us to be involved in being instruments of bringing His healing power to others. The Bible makes that very clear.

I also believe that God's chief desire and ultimate purpose for His children is to conform them to the likeness of His Son. And that may not always include physical healing. We will look at that subject in another chapter.

Do we really believe *"Jesus Christ is the same yesterday and today and forever"* (Hebrews 13:8)?

Let us look at some Scriptures related to healing.

A. From the life and ministry of the Lord Jesus.

"When Jesus had called the Twelve together, he gave them power and authority to drive out all demons and to cure diseases, and he sent them out to preach the kingdom of God and to heal the sick" (Luke 9:1-2).

Some of the Ways of God in Healing

"Jesus went through all the towns and villages, teaching in their synagogues, preaching the good news of the kingdom and healing every disease and sickness" (Matthew 9:35).

"After this the Lord appointed seventy-two others and sent them two by two ahead of him to every town and place where he was about to go" (Luke 10:1).

"Heal the sick who are there and tell them, 'The kingdom of God is near you'" (Luke 10:9).

B. From the example of continued healings, which resulted from the disciples' ministries after Jesus' death and resurrection.

"Then Peter said, 'Silver or gold I do not have, but what I have I give you. In the name of Jesus Christ of Nazareth, walk.' Taking him by the right hand, he helped him up, and instantly the man's feet and ankles became strong. He jumped to his feet and began to walk. Then he went with them into the temple courts, walking and jumping, and praising God" (Acts 3:6-8).

C. Through the life and teachings of Paul.

"God did extraordinary miracles through Paul, so that even handkerchiefs and aprons that had touched him were taken to the sick, and their illnesses were cured and the evil spirits left them" (Acts 19:11-12).

"...to another gifts of healing by that one Spirit" (I Corinthians 12:9).

D. From the exhortation of James.

"Is any one of you sick? He should call the elders of the church to pray over him and anoint him with oil in the name of the Lord. And the prayer offered in faith will make the sick person well; the Lord will raise him up. If he has sinned, he will be forgiven. Therefore confess your sins to each other and pray for each other so that you may

be healed. *The prayer of a righteous man is powerful and effective"* (James 5:14-16).

We would be unwise to quickly claim God's healing power without first recognizing and fulfilling the conditions needed to make the claim.

One morning I was teaching at a Youth With A Mission School of Evangelism in Switzerland. I had been teaching morning and night for weeks and had been in perfect health. It was about the third or fourth week, in the middle of winter, when I woke up one morning shivering with cold, although the room was heated. I was nauseated and felt ill. I longed to stay in bed and just sleep.

I realized that I needed to have clear direction from God as to whether I was to follow the dictates of my legitimate desires, or to carry on with God's mandate to teach.

So I obeyed God's counsel, *"Trust in the Lord with all your heart and lean not on your own understanding; in all your ways acknowledge him, and he will make your paths straight"* (Proverbs 3:5-6).

I was also aware of the ability of demonic powers to put an impression into my mind to keep me from doing God's will. In case they were active, I resisted them in the all-powerful name of the Lord Jesus Christ and believed that they were silenced, according to James 4:7 *"Submit yourselves, then to God. Resist the devil and he will flee from you."*

Although the Lord had not yet shown me what I was to teach that morning, I said, "Lord, do you want me to go out there and give the word of the Lord to the students?" An impression came into my mind, "Go, I will strengthen you." I thought, "All right, that's that." So I started to get dressed, but then I felt worse.

I thought, "How in the world can I even concentrate to seek God from His Word to get the word of the Lord this morning? Maybe I received a wrong impression." So I got down on my knees and went through the whole process again and listened. I heard the voice of the Lord in my spirit say, "Go, I will sustain you." I said, "OK, that's definitely it."

I had nothing to eat or drink, finished dressing, had no idea what the message was, and made it into the classroom. I was too weak that morning to stand, so I sat on a stool, bowed my head in prayer and started praising God for who He is in His glory and power. I thanked Him in faith that He was going to give us a remarkable morning and praised God for the privilege of being there. Then I thanked Him that He was going to tell me what to do. I prayed that there would be a mighty move of God's Spirit and I released faith.

God directed me to share about aspects of His character and enabled me to teach with authority. God's power was also evident upon the students as they responded to fresh revelation. It was a mighty time that could only be explained by God. In the midst of it I was completely healed and actually given such supernatural energy of mind and body, I felt as though I could have climbed Mt. Everest— well, almost!

The move of God's Spirit lasted until 1:00 p.m. I then immediately joined Loren Cunningham, the director of the school, at his request, to help deal with a complex situation involving a student. God's wisdom and strength continued to flow to meet that need. About mid-afternoon I stopped to eat and drink, feeling as fit as a trout swimming upstream!

Unconditional obedience became the key to the release of God's healing power.

Soon after Moses led the children of Israel out of Egypt, God gave them this promise, "...*If you will diligently hearken to the voice of the Lord your God, and do that which is right in his eyes and give heed to his commandments and keep all his statutes, I will put none of the diseases upon you which I put upon the Egyptians; for I am the Lord, your healer*" (Exodus 15:26 RSV).

What was the condition to the promise "...*I am the Lord your healer...*"? Obedience.

Let's look at that verse more closely. "*If you will diligently [not casually] hearken to the voice of the Lord your God and do that which is right in his eyes,*" (not just the eyes of men). Now how can we know what is right in His eyes? There is only one way. We must search the Scriptures to see what His standard of righteousness is. "*And give heed to his commandments and keep all his statutes.*" That means being obedient to revealed truth and the promptings of the Holy Spirit. Then He says, "*I will put none of the diseases upon you which I put upon the Egyptians.*"

What is God saying here? He *did* put disease upon some people. But He said, "I won't do that if you will diligently hearken to Me and obey Me. Then you will prove that I am the Lord your Healer."

In Psalm 103:2-3 we read, "*Praise the Lord, O my soul, and forget not all his benefits—who forgives all your sins and heals all your diseases.*"

What would you think of somebody who went around claiming, "God forgives all my sins. The Bible says so. I take it from Psalm 103:2-3. I committed adultery last week, and God has forgiven me. I've lied. He's forgiven me. It doesn't matter what I've done, the Bible says He forgives me. 'Praise the Lord, O my soul, and forget not all His benefits.' I'm living in the forgiveness of God"?

We know perfectly well there wouldn't be an ounce of forgiveness from God unless that person had turned from the sin that he or she was committing in real repentance. *Then* God would forgive. So there is a definite condition, isn't there? But often people take the part of this verse related to healing and claim it, without seeking God to see if there are conditions to be fulfilled first.

We cannot build a doctrine around an isolated verse of Scripture. Scriptures must be in harmony with other Scriptures on a given subject to arrive at truth. Each truth must also be based upon the character of God, and the principles by which God operates as revealed in the whole of God's Word.

Then in Isaiah 53:4-5 (RSV) we read the prophecy about the Lord Jesus. *"Surely he has borne our griefs [or sicknesses] and carried our sorrows [or pains]; yet we esteemed him stricken, smitten by God, and afflicted. But he was wounded for our transgressions, he was bruised for our iniquities; upon him was the chastisement that made us whole, and with his stripes we are healed."*

It is clear from these Scriptures that our beloved Savior took the punishment for our sins and suffered for our sicknesses that we may become whole. But in order for His atoning work upon the cross to be appropriated in our lives and for us to become His children, there are definite steps we need to take. (See the section at the end of this book titled "What a Committal of Life to the Lord Jesus Christ Means.")

It is also important for us to understand that before we claim physical healing on the basis of the above Scriptures, it would be wise for us to seek God if that is His will and purpose at that particular time in our lives.

"Who can speak and have it happen if the Lord has not decreed it?" (Lamentations 3:37)

The next chapter will help us to know how to pray in order to get the right answers to meet our deepest needs.

3

Four Key Prayers

If we, or someone else with whom we are involved, need healing, be it mental, spiritual, physical or emotional, there are four very important prayers we can pray and release faith at the end of every prayer. Because if we do not believe God is going to answer us, nothing is going to happen, according to Hebrews 11:6, *"And without faith it is impossible to please God..."* And then in Romans 14, the last part of verse 23 says, *"...And everything that does not come from faith is sin."* And again Hebrews 3:12 says, *"See to it, brothers, that none of you has a sinful, unbelieving heart that turns away from the living God."*

Always start with worshiping and praising God for *Who He is.* This gives reason to praise Him under every circumstance, and praise releases God's power.

Some of the Ways of God in Healing

The first prayer is, *"Dear God, do something in these circumstances that will bring the maximum glory to Your name."*

That's the prayer that will cause God's hand to be moved more than any other. And yet that's often the last prayer that God hears when we are sick. Many times we have tried everything we know to be healed and then finally say, "Well God, just do something that will bring glory to Your name." And that's the moment when God starts to act. Sound familiar?

In Catherine Marshall's marvelous book, *Beyond Ourselves*, we read about the time when she had tuberculosis for two years and had been doing everything to be healed, including much praying. Finally she said something like, "Lord, I relinquish myself into Your hands. Do anything that will bring glory to Your name."

And then it happened. The Lord Jesus came and manifested Himself to her in her bedroom. She felt His presence and knew that He was sitting beside her, had touched her and healed her. He had been waiting all that time for her to get to the place where all that mattered was that glory came to His name in His way and time through her circumstances. When we are truly at that place, it won't matter to us whether we are healed or not. We leave that decision to an all-wise, all-loving God.

The fact that our requests to God should always be motivated by a primary desire for His glory is highlighted in John 14:13, *"And I will do whatever you ask in my name, so that the Son may bring glory to the Father."*

The second prayer we need to pray is, *"Please tell me what it is You're trying to teach me at this time. Thank You that You will."* Not, "Teach the other person."

Perhaps you have the responsibility for praying for one who is sick. It may be a family member or a friend, and you have no understanding why healing doesn't come. Well, ask God what it is He's trying to teach you. Or you may be the one who needs the healing. The more deeply involved we are, the more we need to pray that prayer, and believe God will answer.

The third prayer is, *"In Your way, and in Your time, please reveal to me the purposes and/or the causes of this illness. Thank You that You will."*

It is often more important to have answers to these last two questions than it is to be healed.

When we have understanding about how our sickness fits into God's overall plan for our lives, we can accept the circumstance and then expect God to use it for His glory and our good.

We are also going to come out of our suffering with a lot more understanding of God's ways.

The fourth prayer is, *"Tell me the next thing that I am to do. Thank You that You will, in Your way and in Your time."*

Now, there's nothing complicated about that. As we diligently seek God, He will fulfill His promises to make clear to us our next steps. *"I will instruct you and teach you in the way you should go; I will counsel you and watch over you"* (Psalm 32:8).

"But as for me, I will look to the Lord, I will wait for the God of my salvation; my God will hear me" (Micah 7:7 RSV).

We now have things in their right perspective and God is released to go into action.

You will find many stories throughout this book that relate to the last three prayers.

GOD'S SOVEREIGNTY

In whichever way God works and however God answers us, we should always remember the sovereignty of God. *"See now that I myself am He! There is no god besides me. I put to death and I bring to life, I have wounded and I will heal, and no one can deliver out of my hand"* (Deuteronomy 32:39).

We can't twist God's arm to try and get Him to do something we want Him to do. God is waiting for us to have the maturity to come to the point where we pray these kinds of prayers that are according to His character and His ways.

We need to understand that in God's sovereignty, He is absolutely righteous. He is absolutely just. *"The Lord is just in all his ways, and kind in all his doings"* (Psalm 145:17 RSV). *"He is the Rock, his works are perfect, and all his ways are just. A faithful God who does no wrong, upright and just is he"* (Deuteronomy 32:4).

In Ezekiel 14:23 we read *"'...I have not done without cause all that I have done in it,' says the Lord God"* (RSV). God always has a reason for what He has allowed to happen to us. He is not a capricious God, and He is not an unkind God. He is a loving God who is working out a plan for our ultimate good.

4

God's Ultimate Purpose for His Children

God makes it very clear in Romans 8:29 that His ultimate purpose for us is to be conformed to the image of His Son, the Lord Jesus Christ. That is the ultimate purpose for our obtaining salvation through the commitment of our lives to Him.

Romans 8:28 tells us that to those who love the Lord (and love for Him is measured by obedience to Him, John 14:15) and are called according to His purpose, we can know for sure that God is working out a plan that will be for our good in *all* our circumstances.

What we are apt to forget is that when the circumstances are difficult and painful, including ill health or accidental injury, they fit right into God's all-wise, perfect plan to help achieve His ultimate goal for us.

Also, that's often when some of the devil's most subtle suggestions come to our minds—that we're useless and therefore can't be used by God for the extension of His Kingdom.

At the same time, we can easily make excuses for ourselves and think that we are not responsible or accountable to God to have an effective ministry to others because of the limitations of our physical condition.

The truth is that in the process of becoming more like the Lord Jesus Christ, complete healing in this life may or may not be included in God's perfect plan.

However, because there is so much in God's Word to encourage us to ask God to heal us, provided we fulfill His conditions, we can expect that many times He will, in His way and time. But if He doesn't, we can rest assured that He has a better plan that includes the extension of His Kingdom through us *without limitations!*

God is unlimited in power through a totally surrendered, clean, obedient, believer who is filled with the Holy Spirit. An effective worldwide ministry can result even when healing is withheld.

What better example is there of this truth than Joni Eareckson Tada, known and loved by multitudes. Although paralyzed from the shoulders down, confined to her wheelchair, God vividly manifests the life of His Son through her continuously.

At the age of seventeen, Joni was paralyzed through a diving accident. She came to embrace God's justice, sovereignty, wisdom and love as irrevocable realities toward her, and has continued to do the next thing He has told her to do. As a result, in the ensuing years God has enabled her to do the following, with dedicated helpers:

- Write twelve books.

- Become an accomplished artist, through holding her pen and paint brush between her teeth.

- Play the role of herself in a movie that World Wide Pictures (part of the Billy Graham Organization) made about her life.

- Speak at national and international conferences.

- Speak on a five-minute daily radio program since 1982, airing more than 700 times daily around the world.

- Head up an organization called "Joni and Friends," which accelerates ministry to disabled persons in the Christian community. This includes encouraging the disabled and their families to pursue worthwhile goals.

In her own words, Joni says, "However, even if I were paralyzed and relegated to a back bedroom, unable to paint, write or speak, I could still have a worldwide ministry through encouragement, intercession and obedience."

It is important to know that Joni believes wholeheartedly in God's miraculous ability to heal people today. But she says, "We can rest in God's sovereign purpose and design to bring glory to Himself, whether it's through full health or through our suffering."

There are a number of reasons why suffering in some degree is a necessary part of our lives.

One purpose is to produce endurance, and endurance produces character (Romans 5:3-4).

Another purpose is that we may be able to minister understanding and compassion to others who suffer (II Corinthians 1:4).

We may well have to suffer as we obey God's command to take the Good News to all creation. Also, the Lord Jesus told us we were to deny ourselves and take up our cross and follow Him (Luke 9:23).

Then there is the inevitable suffering that comes to us all from living in a fallen world. The sin of mankind over thousands of years has produced a polluted world that is very far removed from the one in which God intended man to live.

Now let's look at some of the causes of sickness.

5

A Possible Cause of Sickness

Cause one: *This can be an attack of Satan and demon powers*, allowed by God to give the opportunity for a demonstration of the far greater power of God over the enemy as we take authority over him.

We need to come against the powers of darkness with the fourfold weapons of our warfare, which the Bible says "*...are not the weapons of the world. On the contrary, they have divine power to demolish strongholds*" (II Corinthians 10:4). They are the Holy Spirit, the Word of God, the name of the Lord Jesus Christ and the blood of the Lord Jesus. It means being filled with the Holy Spirit, wielding the sword of the Spirit, which is the Word of God—quoting the "it is writtens" against Satan as Jesus did, then presenting to the enemy the precious shed blood of the Lord Jesus, which represents all His victories on the Cross. We also declare Satan's defeat in the all-powerful name of the Lord Jesus Christ.

Some of the Ways of God in Healing

How can we tell if Satan is the cause of the sickness? We need to say something like this as we test the situation:

> Satan, principalities and demon powers, I stand against you in the mighty name of the Lord Jesus Christ. It is written, "...*the one who is in you is greater than the one who is in the world*" (I John 4:4). You cannot put anything on me (or the person that we're praying for) other than what God would allow for my good. I bind you according to the Word of God, "...*Whatever you bind on earth will be bound in Heaven...*" (Matthew 18:18). I resist you. It is written, "...*Resist the devil, and he will flee from you*" (James 4:7). It is written, "*They overcame him [Satan] by the blood of the Lamb and by the word of their testimony...*" (Revelation 12:11). If you're the cause of the sickness, in Jesus' name, I loose myself (or that person) from all satanic attack.

We then praise and worship God for His all-surpassing power over the enemy of our souls. "*Praise be to the Lord, my Rock, who trains my hands for war, my fingers for battle. He is my loving God and my fortress, my stronghold and my deliverer, my shield, in whom I take refuge, who subdues peoples under me*" (Psalm 144:1-2).

Now if it is an attack of Satan, and we have faith in these spiritual weapons, what's going to happen? We are going to start to become well! As we continue to praise God for who He is, that depression is going to lift. That dissension in our family is going to cease. That pain in the back is going to go!

A Possible Cause of Sickness

In Luke 13:11 we read, *"And a woman was there who had been crippled by a spirit for eighteen years. She was bent over and could not straighten up at all."* In verse 16 Jesus says, *"Then should not this woman, a daughter of Abraham, whom Satan has kept bound for eighteen long years, be set free on the Sabbath day from what bound her?"* Her sickness was caused by a satanic bondage and Jesus freed her from it.

One Sunday afternoon, I was interceding for a missionary organization, other than the one to which I belong. There was a relationship problem among the missionaries in leadership, and I was praying for it to be solved. I came against the powers of darkness by commanding, in Jesus' name, the cessation of all satanic activity arrayed against these men. I continued in intensive spiritual warfare until I sensed the battle was won.

I had just gotten up off my knees when a violent pain gripped me in my throat. I've never felt anything like it before or since. It felt as if a power inside my throat was pulling my head backward. Instantly I knew that it was a satanic attack on my body in relation to the spiritual warfare that had been waged in intercession.

I said, "Satan, principalities, and demon powers, greater is He who is in me—the living Lord Jesus Christ—than you who are in the world. You have no power over my body. Loose your grip on my throat at this instant in Jesus' mighty name." Immediately my head came forward and the pain gradually subsided. It was a violent, quick thing.

However, I didn't have a moment's fear. I knew where that force was coming from, and I don't fear one who is nothing but a fallen angel doomed to eternal destruction. Nor do I fear his emissaries. I fear God, who created the heavens and the earth. And when we fear the Lord, we don't fear men or demons.

If the problem continues, what have we learned? The cause was not the devil or his demons. I find Christians all over the world acting as though the devil was omnipresent. The minute something goes wrong, they immediately blame him.

In many cases, this is the easy way out, excusing the person from any personal responsibility. Satan is not everywhere. He can't be. He is not omnipresent, nor are his emissaries. Don't attribute that kind of power to them. That's why we need to understand that there can be other causes and purposes for sickness.

6

It's Not Always the Devil

A second cause for sickness can be sin in our lives. Either we're conscious of it, and we resist the promptings of the Holy Spirit to humble ourselves and repent, or we're not conscious of it, and God reveals it to us when we press in with the key questions already stated. We simply say, "Lord, is undealt-with sin the cause of this sickness? If it is, I truly want to repent of it." This kind of earnest, honest inquiry frees the Holy Spirit to bring the necessary revelation. God will reward the diligent, persistent seeker (Hebrews 11:6).

The following passage from Psalms makes it clear that God can use sickness, whether spiritual, emotional, mental or physical to get our attention when repentance is needed. *"Some were sick through their sinful ways, and because of their iniquities suffered affliction"* (Psalm 107:17 RSV).

It hurts God more to discipline us than it does for us to be disciplined. He is a God of unfathomable love.

Listen to His heart: *"Though he brings grief, he will show compassion, so great is his unfailing love. For he does not willingly bring affliction or grief to the children of men"* (Lamentations 3:32-33).

David says, *"I know, O Lord, that your laws are righteous, and in faithfulness you have afflicted me"* (Psalm 119:75).

He shares a similar testimony in Psalm 32:1-2, *"Blessed is he whose transgressions are forgiven, whose sins are covered. Blessed is the man whose sin the Lord does not count against him and in whose spirit is no deceit."*

Then he explains in verses 3-5, *"When I kept silent, my bones wasted away through my groaning all day long. For day and night your hand was heavy upon me; my strength was sapped as in the heat of summer. Then I acknowledged my sin to you and did not cover up my iniquity. I said, 'I will confess my transgressions to the Lord.'—And you forgave the guilt of my sin."*

It's obvious that sin was the cause of his suffering and that the judgment of God was manifest in David's body. But when he repented of his sin, God mercifully forgave him.

In Numbers 11:4-33 we read of the children of Israel murmuring because they didn't have meat, and God gave them meat, but punished them for their murmuring. Verse 33 *"But while the meat was still between their teeth and before it could be consumed, the anger of the Lord burned against the people, and he struck them with a severe plague."*

Paul was strong in his rebuke to the Corinthian believers in relation to their behavior, when they celebrated the Lord's Supper. The cause was disunity, selfishness and drunkenness, along with a casual attitude toward the implications of participating in the Communion service.

Paul makes it very clear that God's judgment had been manifest in their bodies. Many were weak, and sick, and a number had even died (I Corinthians 11:17-34).

In John 5:1-14 we read about the man who had been ill for 38 years and was sitting by the pool, hoping for healing. Jesus came to him and said, *"Get up! Pick up your mat and walk."* And then later He said this very significant thing, *"See, you are well again. Stop sinning or something worse may happen to you."* In effect Jesus was saying, "You and I know perfectly well that the cause of this sickness was sin. I've healed you, but don't go back to the sin, or the judgment will be worse."

Galatians 6:7-8 says *"Do not be deceived: God cannot be mocked. A man reaps what he sows. The one who sows to please his sinful nature, from that nature will reap destruction; the one who sows to please the Spirit, from the Spirit will reap eternal life."* In other words, when we sin with our bodies, we will suffer in our bodies. It's a fixed law of God; what we sow, we reap. But, praise God, we can shorten the inevitable reaping period through humbling ourselves before God and man. Mercy is always extended to a truly repentant heart. We can ask for it, and others can ask for it on our behalf.

I was in another country teaching each morning and evening for a week. The spiritual leader and his wife were driving me home from one of the meetings, accompanied by a young married woman who had heard four of my messages. There was strong emphasis in them on the need to get to know God in order to make Him known—and that there are no shortcuts to knowing Him. She heard that it takes time alone with God daily, seeking to know His character and His ways from His Word, plus having an effective prayer life for others.

I knew nothing about this young woman, other than her first name. As we stopped to let her out of the car, she turned and said to the driver, "Would you pray for me? I have a splitting headache." He said, "Sure." Just as quickly, he turned to me and said, "Joy, would you pray for her?" I did not have the instantaneous witness to pray for her healing. (I sometimes do, and I sometimes don't.) So I said, "God, have You anything to say or pray through me for this woman?"

After a little time, God said to me, "Ask her if she is prepared to ask the million dollar question." Well, now, God and I know what that is, so I said to her, "Do you want to learn what God is trying to teach you? And do you want to learn it more than you want this splitting headache to be lifted?" Finally she said, "Yes, I guess I do." I said, "I suggest you ask Him that question now."

There was a long time of silence. I presumed she was cooperating. And then I said, "Well, Lord, have You anything else that You want to say to me in relation to this woman?" Here is the simple prayer that He gave me for her.

"Dear God, in the name of the Lord Jesus, I bring her to You and I ask that right now You would meet the deepest need of her mind, body, soul and spirit, as You see it to be. Thank You that You're doing it. Amen." She just said, "Thank you, good night," and went into her house.

The next morning, she said, "Joy, I've got a story to tell you. I didn't tell you last night in what bad shape I was, but I was at the end of my rope. I had had that splitting headache for three weeks, and it didn't matter how many pain-killing tablets I took, I could get no relief. I was also on tranquilizers to try and cope, as I have a four-year-old son to look after. What really baffled me was that in the last two days of attending these meetings, it got worse! I knew I needed help.

"When I said to God, in the back seat of that car last night, 'I want to know what it is You're trying to teach me more than I want this headache to be lifted,' He spoke very clearly into my mind and said, 'You have disobeyed Me repeatedly over the years. I've spoken to you directly and indirectly, and told you to have time alone with Me in the Word of God on a disciplined, daily basis in order to get to know Me. I've told you to take time aside daily to pray for others.' He continued, 'You'll serve Me in other ways, but refuse to obey Me in these areas. You've been exposed to a lot more truth in the last two days about these priorities, and you still won't get alone with Me.'"

She went on to tell me that she responded quietly in her heart, "Oh God, it's so true. I not only confess it tonight, I repent. I tell You that from tonight on, I will make having time alone with You a priority in my life." Then she said, "Immediately after that, you said, 'Thank You, Lord Jesus, that You are meeting the deepest need in this dear woman's heart and life right at this moment.' Instantly I was released from the pressure of what felt like a burning band around my head. It then felt as though a cool ice pack had replaced it. I got out of that car healed."

When she told me this story, I asked, "Are you prepared to get up tonight in front of these people and give testimony of some of the ways of God in sickness and healing?" She did, and her text to precede her testimony was, *"I know, O Lord, that your laws are righteous, and in faithfulness you have afflicted me"* (Psalm 119:75). She said, "God is just in all His ways and kind in all His doings. I'm so glad to be freed now to be an obedient servant of God." There was no healing for that woman until there was repentance of the sin of disobedience that had been the cause.

"Do not be wise in your own eyes; fear the Lord and shun evil. This will bring health to your body and nourishment to your bones" (Proverbs 3:7-8).

We need to understand the meaning of the fear of the Lord. Proverbs 8:13 says it is to hate sin. We don't choose to do the things we hate, unless forced to by a higher authority. It means more than refraining from sin because sin is wrong, or because the consequences of it are too great. It means we choose not to sin because we *hate* it. It also means to stand in awe of God's holiness.

We need to often ask God to give us His attitude toward sin, and believe that He will. He will put the fear of God on us, which will be the strongest incentive not to sin. *"...Through the fear of the Lord a man avoids evil"* (Proverbs 16:6).

The sin of unbelief in God's ability can also stop the healing power of God. In Matthew 13:58 we read that Jesus *"...did not do many miracles there because of their lack of faith."*

If we lack compassion for people who are not well, God can cause or allow an illness in us, to correct that character weakness. That has been the experience of two of my close friends. Perhaps we've been judgmental, and have lacked compassion for an individual who has suffered...until we found ourselves suffering in the same way. On one occasion, this was my experience.

The Ten Commandments are not ten suggestions. They are God's moral absolutes. One of them states that we are to take one day in seven to rest from our regular duties. *"Six days you shall labor and do all your work, but the seventh day is a Sabbath to the Lord your God"* (Deuteronomy 5:13,14).

God rested on the seventh day, after creating the universe (Genesis 2:2). This was not because He had run out of energy. It is to remind us that we, in our humanity, need to have the refreshing that can only come through obedience to this command.

If we think we know better than God, and choose to disobey, in time, we will reap the inevitable consequences in our bodies.

Praise God that His mercy is always extended to a truly repentant heart. *"Blessed is the man whom God corrects; so do not despise the discipline of the Almighty. For he wounds, but he also binds up; he injures, but his hands also heal"* (Job 5:17-18).

HEAVIER JUDGMENT FOR LEADERS

In Numbers 12 we find God putting leprosy on Miriam because of her sins of criticism and jealousy of her brother Moses. It is very significant that when the greatest intercessor/leader of the Old Testament, Moses, cried out to God to heal his sister Miriam, God did not answer his prayer until she had been isolated from the people for at least a week...all very humbling. Everybody in the camp would have to know that Miriam was under God's judgment because verse 15 says "*...and the people did not move on till she was brought back.*"

Why the severity of judgment, and why would everyone need to know about it?

The first reason is that she was in a position of authority and influence as a prophetess/leader. "*...I sent Moses to lead you, also Aaron and Miriam*" (Micah 6:4).

God is showing us that the greater the level of spiritual leadership and ministry responsibilities, plus the revelation of truth that He gives us, the greater responsibility we have to live that truth. Then if we fail, we have greater accountability and judgment from God. That's justice.

God is at work to remove hypocrisy from the lives of spiritual leaders. "*Not many of you should presume to be teachers, my brothers, because you know that we who teach will be judged more strictly*" (James 3:1).

When we are *real*, we provoke others to be real by the godly influence that emanates from our lives. When we are *not* real, we tempt others to follow us in our hypocrisy. God severely judges hypocrisy in spiritual leaders, because it is abhorrent to Him. We know this from Jesus' strong reaction to the hypocritical spiritual leaders when He was on earth.

The second reason is that God wants to show us the gravity in His sight of the sins of criticism and jealousy, especially when they are against the Lord's anointed. *"Do not touch my anointed ones, do my prophets no harm"* (Psalm 105:15). Miriam broke that command.

How pointless it would have been for Miriam to have been claiming healing when she was under the judgment of God! When the period of reaping the results of her sins was over, God in His mercy must have healed her, because we read that she returned to the camp and then all the people moved on (Numbers 12:15-16).

The same sin of criticizing the Lord's anointed leader was committed by Michal, David's wife. She despised David in her heart, and spoke disrespectfully and critically to him when he came home from a great victory, praising God with singing and dancing. She had a barren womb for the rest of her life, so was childless under the judgment of God.

What is God showing us? First, His perspective on her sin. And second, that *much* understanding brings *much* responsibility. She lived with the man who lived and taught, "Don't touch the Lord's anointed." David could have killed Saul on more than one occasion, but he chose not to. The Bible says, *"...David was conscience-stricken..."* (I Samuel 24:5) just for cutting off a piece of Saul's robe. In other words, Michal was exposed to the truth of "don't touch the Lord's anointed" probably more than any other wife we know of in God's Word. God's justice was manifest in the judgment she received.

Then there is King Uzziah in II Chronicles 26:16-21. He became proud and stepped outside his sphere of ministry and started to do what only the priests had been called to do. When he was rebuked by them, he became angry. *"...And when he became angry with the priests leprosy broke out on his forehead....And they thrust him out quickly, and he himself hastened to go out...."* Now note the words that follow, *"...because the Lord had smitten him"* (RSV).

In II Chronicles 21:18-19 we read about King Jehoram, *"After all this, the Lord afflicted Jehoram with an incurable disease of the bowels. In the course of time, at the end of the second year, his bowels came out because of the disease, and he died in great pain...."* This judgment on his body was the result of a life of much sin.

All these Scriptures should be sufficient proof that sin can be a cause of sickness, and that God can use sickness as a form of discipline.

However, remember John 9:1-3 *"As he went along, he saw a man blind from birth. His disciples asked him, 'Rabbi, who sinned, this man or his parents, that he was born blind?' 'Neither this man nor his parents sinned,' said Jesus, 'but this happened so that the work of God might be displayed in his life.'"*

We must be very careful not to wrongly judge by presumption. We should not look at people and quickly say, "I know that the cause of their sickness is sin. They need to repent!"

It's Not Always the Devil

Don't look at someone and say, "All you need is faith." Let God be the judge. But we should encourage ourselves and others to seek God for an understanding of the cause of our disorders.

7

The Importance of Forgiveness

Medical science recognizes the connection between resentment and some illnesses. For example, resentment has been known at times to be the cause of high blood pressure, ulcers, rashes, headaches, arthritis and an inability to function sexually in marriage.

Resentment is a strongly destructive force to our minds, bodies, souls and spirits. *"A heart at peace gives life to the body, but envy rots the bones"* (Proverbs 14:30). Job 5:2 is even stronger, *"Resentment kills a fool...."*

Many times our wholeness is dependent upon our choosing to forgive others who have wronged and hurt us.

Once when I was teaching on how to hear God's voice, a girl in her late teens asked God why she was always sick. He responded by convicting her of her resentment to her mother. She repented deeply of that sin and asked God's forgiveness. Then she heard the Holy Spirit speaking into her mind the words, "Turn to Jeremiah chapter 30 and verse 17." She hadn't a clue what that verse was, but looked it up. To her amazement and delight, she read, "*'But I will restore you to health and heal your wounds,' declares the Lord....*" She claimed that promise by faith, and was healed.

God is able to release His ability to forgive others to every heart that believes His Word. "*See to it that no one misses the grace of God and that no bitter root grows up to cause trouble and defile many*" (Hebrews 12:15).

The following are some powerful steps, that when applied, always produce the grace of God spoken of in that verse.

1. If we have repented of sins we have committed, we must receive God's forgiveness (I John 1:9). On that basis we must also forgive ourselves. It will be difficult to forgive others if we haven't.

2. We must realize that forgiving others is an act of the will. We have to desire it and then choose it. True forgiveness means that we will not *want* to tell others about the person who wronged us. "*...love covers over [not exposes] a multitude of sins*" (I Peter 4:8).

3. We must also realize that we will not be forgiven by God unless we forgive others.

"*For if you forgive men when they sin against you, your heavenly Father will also forgive you. But if you do not forgive men their sins, your Father will not forgive your sins*" (Matthew 6:14-15).

4. Realize that our prayers are ineffective if we have resentment in our hearts. Notice the link between *forgiveness* and *prayer* in Matthew 6:12. When Jesus instructs the disciples how to pray, He says, *"Forgive us our debts, as we also have forgiven our debtors."*

Again in Mark 11:25, *"And when you stand praying, if you hold anything against anyone, forgive him, so that your Father in heaven may forgive you your sins."*

Now notice the link between forgiveness and faith when we pray. Verse 24 *"...Whatever you ask for in prayer, believe that you have received it, and it will be yours."* Then comes verse 25, warning us to forgive anyone who has hurt us or wronged us.

> *"So watch yourselves. If your brother sins, rebuke him, and if he repents, forgive him. If he sins against you seven times in a day, and seven times comes back to you and says, 'I repent,' forgive him." The apostles said to the Lord, "Increase our faith!" He replied, "If you have faith as small as a mustard seed, you can say to this mulberry tree, 'Be uprooted and planted in the sea,' and it will obey you"* (Luke 17:3-6).

Job had to forgive his friends for their wrong judgment of him before he could pray effectively for them. *"After Job had prayed for his friends, the Lord made him prosperous again and gave him twice as much as he had before"* (Job 42:10).

5. Think carefully of all God has forgiven us, and thank Him for His great mercy toward us.

"Be kind and compassionate to one another, forgiving each other, just as in Christ God forgave you" (Ephesians 4:32).

Some of the Ways of God in Healing

"Bear with each other and forgive whatever griev-ances you may have against one another. Forgive as the Lord forgave you" (Colossians 3:13).

God forgives us instantly, joyfully and wholly.

6. Thank the Lord for any or all of the blessings He has brought to us through the people who have hurt us. It is difficult for resentment to remain in a truly grateful heart.

7. Think of the needs of the people at the time they hurt us—the needs of their minds, bodies, souls and spirits. Think of their pressures, responsibilities and difficult circumstances. Their needs then, and now, were probably greater than ours.

8. Ask God to come upon us by His Spirit and give us His supernatural ability to love them and forgive them. *"...God has poured out his love into our hearts by the Holy Spirit, whom he has given us"* (Romans 5:5).

Receive this by faith: *"And without faith it is im-possible to please God, because anyone who comes to him must believe that he exists and that he rewards those who earnestly seek him"* (Hebrews 11:6).

9. Ask God to give us opportunities of expressing His love to them both in word and deed.

"If anyone has material possessions and sees his brother in need but has no pity on him, how can the love of God be in him? Dear children, let us not love with words or tongue but with actions and in truth" (I John 3:17,18).

10. Become an intercessor for them. Pray regu-larly for God to bless, encourage, comfort and strengthen them, and meet their deepest needs.

"But I tell you: Love your enemies and pray for those who persecute you" (Matthew 5:44).

God tells us in Galatians 5:5 that faith works through love.

Thank and praise God for His power that delivers us from resentment. When we do our part, He does His.

Forgiveness not only releases us from destructive forces, but it helps to release the power of God through us to others.

Jesus looked at Peter *with forgiveness* after he had denied the Lord three times, and it melted Peter to repentance.

Jesus addressed Judas as "friend" when he came to betray Him to the chief priests. Obviously this was a loving, loyal greeting, devoid of resentment.

Both the Lord Jesus and Stephen made forgiveness a way of life. That is why at their deaths they could intercede to the Father for mercy to be extended to their murderers...the ultimate in forgiveness.

Whom are We to Forgive?

We are to forgive only those we are sure have wronged us. We must be careful not to presume that because we're feeling hurt, someone is necessarily guilty of an offense toward us. The person through whom the hurt came may be totally unaware of having hurt us.

Perhaps our pride has been hurt. We need to ask God to reveal to us why we are feeling resentful. The answers to that question could give us an understanding of how to avoid being unnecessarily hurt again. We may have brought on the painful circumstances through a lack of wisdom.

We always suffer the most to the extent that we love the person who has hurt us, and where injustice is involved. Therefore, the ones we need to forgive the most are often those closest to us.

Let us check through this list for any hidden resentments: parents, husbands, wives, children, grandchildren, brothers, sisters, other relatives, friends, school teachers, spiritual leaders, people we've been teamed with in ministry, people under our authority or over us in authority, politicians and government officials from our own nation or other nations.

It is significant to note that unless Hannah had immediately forgiven Eli (her priest) when he misjudged her so badly in I Samuel 1:12-14, she would not have received the pronounced blessing through him...which was a healing of years of barrenness!

The more we experience injustice, the more we are tempted to resent the perpetrator. Therefore, we need to check our reactions in the presence of the Lord during our painful experiences.

In Youth With A Mission (the missionary organization with which I am associated), most of our students go on two-month evangelism outreaches following their three-month training courses. Many times this includes going to foreign countries. We also have short-term outreach teams, mostly in the summer months. The following illustration comes into that category.

One of our staff (whom I shall call Mary) had negotiated airline bookings with a travel agent for a number of young people who were going on an "Around the World" team. What she didn't know was that the agent had taken their money to help pay back several airlines from whom he had previously stolen money.

After Mary's repeated unsuccessful attempts to get the tickets from him, she learned that he had been caught by the police and sentenced to imprisonment.

This resulted in great stress for Mary, who had to handle this embarrassing and difficult situation with the young people, and, in some cases, their parents. Stress was also put upon some of the team members who found themselves stranded in overseas airports without the tickets being at the airline counters, as promised by the agent.

During many weeks of anxiety, as Mary was involved with all of the resultant complexities, she developed severe, persistent pain in her shoulders, back and legs. Several people told her that her symptoms sounded like the early stages of arthritis.

The financial need was shared over a period of weeks among a number of Christians who rallied to the call. Gradually the total amount needed for every team member was met. *They never reached a destination late, and none of God's purposes were thwarted. Praise God!*

While the team members' problems had been solved, Mary's had not. The pains in her body persisted. When attending a staff prayer meeting, having given a report on all the problems recently associated with this dishonest agent, she overheard a leader praying softly, "Oh Lord, help her to forgive him."

Immediately God convicted her of the sin of resentment, and she repented on the spot. All pain left her body. She was instantly and permanently healed. God made it clear to her that resentment was the cause of her suffering, and repentance brought the cure.

8

Stop Carrying It

Chronic tension in the mind, through not casting our burdens on the Lord and believing He will sustain us, is rooted in the sins of unbelief and disobedience to the Word of God. *"Cast your cares on the Lord and he will sustain you; he will never let the righteous fall"* (Psalm 55:22). So often we keep them to ourselves, murmur, have self-pity and do not roll them on Him. What does that produce? Many times it produces physical, mental and emotional disorders in our bodies.

Psalm 37:5 says, *"Commit your way to the Lord; trust in him, and he will act"* (RSV). The Hebrew word for *commit* is "throw": throw the problem at God. Trust in Him because of who He is, believe He will act, and He will! Obedience to these Scriptures can be the key to many health problems.

A young married woman at a church where I'd spoken, told me that she had had severe pain in her throat for several weeks. Her doctor had examined her, found no physical cause and had recommended that she see a psychiatrist. She had an appointment in a few days.

She had been eating only mashed or sieved foods, and had finally resorted to living on liquids. She was painfully thin when she spoke to me, and asked for my counsel.

When I sought the Lord on her behalf, He directed me to the above Scripture in Psalm 37:5, with the understanding that her problem was related to chronic worry. I explained that she would need to commit (throw) her problems to God.

In order to do that and then trust in Him, she needed to understand His character.

As the God of all power, He would never "miss a catch."

As the God of all the knowledge that is knowable, He knew all about her problems.

As the God of all wisdom, He knew how and when to solve them.

As the God of all righteousness and justice, He would do the right thing for all those connected with the problems.

As the God of all love, He was longing to take her problems. Love's arms hate to be empty.

I suggested that every time she was worried about something, she was to take a cushion in her hand which would represent the cause of concern. Then she was to concentrate on these aspects of God's character and in the light of who He is, *throw* the cushion to Him.

I went on to explain that she could then thank God that He was doing His part. "He will act," I said.

Difficult circumstances that related to her two small children, plus health and financial problems, kept her busy throwing cushions throughout the next day!

When her pastor phoned her home for a progress report she said, "All pain goes, as long as I keep doing my homework on Psalm 37:5."

Her husband was so amazed at the obvious healing in his wife that he decided to act out the Word of God, too.

For weeks he had been hesitant to share with his Christian business associate that he believed God had shown him they were to dissolve their partnership. They had a good relationship, and he was worried about this announcement causing possible misunderstanding and disunity.

At 11 o'clock one night he "threw" his business partner to God, trusted in Him and believed He was acting.

The next morning, before he had time to say anything, his partner approached him and announced that the night before, God had clearly shown him they were to dissolve their partnership and he hoped this would not affect their relationship!

The old hymn says it all:

Oh what peace we often forfeit, Oh what needless pain we bear.

All because we do not carry everything to God in prayer.

But so many times, we carry our burdens into God's presence, talk to Him about them as though

He had no previous knowledge, and then *take them away with us*...and wonder why He doesn't act!

9

Observing God's Natural Laws & Eating for Health

Another cause of sickness can be neglecting to observe God's natural laws for our bodies.

"Do you not know that your body is a temple of the Holy Spirit, who is in you, whom you have received from God? You are not your own; you were bought at a price. Therefore honor (or glorify) God with your body" (I Corinthians 6:19-20).

How can we be glorifying God in our bodies by choosing to put into them things that we know are harmful? These include drugs (apart from those medically prescribed), alcohol, cigarettes, foods that lack nourishment and liquids containing caffeine and tannin.

How can we glorify God in our bodies by overeating, not exercising regularly and persisting in addictions such as sugar in its many forms?

Compulsive eating and drinking habits need to be examined in the light of Paul's testimony *"'All things are lawful for me,' but not all things are helpful. 'All things are lawful for me,' but I will not be enslaved by anything"* (I Corinthians 6:12 RSV).

One day, when I was reading that verse, the Holy Spirit convicted me of being enslaved to drinking tea...which I did all too often. My husband and I were compulsive tea drinkers. We had to admit to God that we were addicted to the caffeine. It was obvious that we needed to repent, which for us meant giving it up completely.

Up until that time, my husband, Jim, quite often had headaches and suffered from what we thought was a sensitive stomach, inherited from his mother. He could not eat fried onions or anything spicy and often had an "acid" stomach. We both had some form of aching joints from time to time, which others in our age group considered to be perfectly normal.

From the day we stopped drinking tea and coffee, all those symptoms disappeared. At the same time, we started having a 50-60 minute brisk walk first thing every morning, combining this with worship and intercession. Later, we made eating low-cholesterol foods a way of life.

The combination of these changes in our daily life style produced a marked improvement in our general health. As I have lived on health foods for most of my life, this meant my going from very good to excellent health.

If we habitually abuse our bodies we will reap the natural consequences.

A man was seen with a T-shirt stretched out of all proportion over his enormous stomach. These words were printed on his shirt, "If I had known I would have lived this long, I would have taken better care of myself."

We know we will experience the results of cause and effect if we neglect to brush our teeth; they will decay. Why are we so slow to realize that the same principle applies when we habitually eat for taste only, and not for health?

Perhaps you're thinking, "I'd hate to give up my favorite foods. They taste so good. Life would be miserable living on foods that are low in fat and without sugar. And as for going without coffee and/or tea—forget it! How would I get going each day and keep going without those boosters?"

I understand that reaction.

Part of the good news is that health foods can be absolutely delicious, and never need to be bland. For many years, I have proven that there's nothing dull about eating the healthy way.

The other part is that when we decide to eat for health, God changes our desires and we find we want only the wholesome foods. The foods that lack nourishment and are not good for us are not even a temptation, because the old cravings are gone.

The fat and sugar content in most of what we consider to be a balanced diet is dangerously high...and the disorders in our bodies are so often the result.

God is not obligated to keep us well and alive, even if we are dedicated servants of His, if we are constantly disobeying His natural and spiritual laws.

Satan tempted Jesus to throw Himself off the highest point of the temple, and quoted Scriptures about God's protection to Him through angels. Jesus answered by quoting the Scripture, *"Do not put the Lord your God to the test"* (Luke 4:12).

We can be "putting the Lord to the test" by choosing to eat foods that medical science has proven to be harmful, acting in presumption and being out of God's will.

Sometimes the cause of sickness is simply that we are experiencing the results of neglecting to heed the warning signals our bodies have been sending us.

How many times have we been disobedient to the promptings of the Holy Spirit in connection with our eating or drinking habits?

I have heard a number of testimonies lately from spiritual leaders, of God's corrective dealings with them in relation to exercise, and adjusted eating and drinking habits. All too frequently it has been connected with some severe physical disorder.

Let's seriously ask the Lord to show us where we are not glorifying God with our bodies, and take the necessary steps of repentance...that means a change of mind, a change of heart and a change of life. *"...I preached that they should repent and turn to God and prove their repentance by their deeds"* (Acts 26:20).

We can also fail to comply with God's natural laws by overtaxing our bodies...whether through lack of sufficient rest or overexertion.

I once pulled the tendons between my shoulders through helping to carry a very heavy mattress. I was in severe discomfort for days, followed by intense pain from muscle spasms.

When I asked God to show me what He wanted to teach me, the understanding came that I had foolishly subjected my body to weights it was never constructed to carry. I learned that lesson the hard way as I had to speak at an Easter service during those days.

Recently I saw on a billboard, "Take care of your body, it's only human!"

Overeating, or eating the wrong foods late at night, can cause indigestion and sleeplessness. Sometimes physical discomforts come from very natural causes.

That reminds me of the anecdote about the man who found he couldn't straighten his back. He went to the doctor for a diagnosis...fearing the worst. The doctor took one look at him and said, "Why don't you take your tie out of your pants zipper?"

In answer to our inquiry as to the cause of a physical disorder, God may lead us to a nutritionist or a doctor who finds that there is a chemical imbalance in our system. Or God may direct us to a physician who finds we need corrective surgery. God has many ways and means of bringing healing to our bodies.

Our part is to take seriously God's words to us, *"Don't you know that you yourselves are God's temple and that God's Spirit lives in you?...God's temple is sacred, and you are that temple"* (I Corinthians 3:16-17).

Section Two

Biblical Purposes for Illness

10

Miracles of Healing

One purpose for illness is to give God an opportunity to demonstrate His mighty power and bring great glory to His name through a miracle of healing. That is an instantaneous healing.

There have to be people in need of miracles before miracles can take place. Have you ever thought of that? *"As he [Jesus] went along, He saw a man blind from birth. His disciples asked Him, 'Rabbi, who sinned, this man or his parents, that he was born blind?' 'Neither this man nor his parents sinned,' said Jesus, 'but this happened so that the work of God might be displayed in his life'"* (John 9:1-3).

In John 11:4 we see the same thing. *"When he heard this [that Lazarus was ill], Jesus said, 'This sickness will not end in death. No, it is for God's glory so that God's Son may be glorified through it.'"*

I'm so glad that we have these clear-cut verses, because they show the other side of the coin of truth.

A lovely athletic Asian girl named Nita Edwards was a student at a university in Sri Lanka when she had an accident which left her totally paralyzed. For a year she lay like a vegetable, her body steadily deteriorating. She couldn't even speak. Pain and medication became routine.

I quote from the book *Miracle in the Mirror*, written about her life by Mark Buntain (veteran missionary to Calcutta, India and now deceased).

> She had trusted the doctors. They had failed.
> She had prayed for God to heal her. He had
> not. In her secret moments, she had even
> prayed to die. That didn't work either.

One day she pled with her pastor, "Why don't you just stop praying for me?" (He had learned to lipread when she needed to communicate.) He replied that he was not going to stop until God had revealed to her the purpose for her life. After that, her prayers changed to, "I'm not asking for healing anymore. I'm not asking to be taken home to heaven. Just tell me what You created me for, and do anything You like with me."

At times she was encouraged from Psalm 31:1, *"In you, O Lord, I have taken refuge...deliver me in your righteousness,"* and Psalm 91:2, *"I will say of the Lord, 'He is my refuge and my fortress, my God, in whom I trust.'"* Other times, she felt an overwhelming sense of emptiness and hopelessness.

It was on one of those days when it happened.

> Suddenly, without warning or fanfare, at
> about four o'clock (in the afternoon) she
> heard a voice. It was a man speaking to her in

a soft, but authoritative tone. It was the most powerful tone she had ever heard.

"Nita, I'm going to raise you up to make you a witness to Asia."

She was startled. If she had been able to, she would have jumped. She had thought she was alone in the room. Where had that voice come from? It said further: "I'm going to heal you on Friday the eleventh of February."

Nita's heart pounded. She was sure no one was in the room. She had never heard that voice before.

But deep in her heart, she already knew she had heard from God; that He had answered her question; that He was going to heal her on Friday, February 11, and that He had answered her question in a completely unique and thoroughly dramatic way.

She later asked God to tell her the time of the day the healing would take place. While God had spoken audibly the first time, He now chose to speak into her spirit with a quiet inner voice, saying that it would be at 3:30 in the afternoon.

She fully believed God, and lived in anticipation of the event with exhilarated joy. She shared it with her pastor, instructing him to have certain people around her bed at the time God had revealed to her, including medical experts for verification of the miracle.

It was minutes before 3:30 p.m. on Friday, February 11.

The power of God invaded the room, from the right side of her bed, like a ball of fire.

Nita's bed began to vibrate with the energy of God's presence, and she felt a million volts of power coursing through her body.

Right on 3:30 p.m., Nita saw a manifestation of the living Christ. He came with a brilliant burst of glory and touched her.

The chains of paralysis exploded away as Nita rocketed out over the end of her bed.

She landed on her knees with a thud.

Her knees had not been bent in over a year; now they were bent before her Jesus. Her hands, useless for so long, were now straightened, upraised, worshipping God. Her voice had been still; now her mouth began to fill with heavenly words, tumbling out in a bubbly fountain of praise. For the first time in her life, she was leading others in prayer.

It is a medical fact that anyone who suffers paralysis in the legs for three months or more, suffers muscular atrophy and must undergo physical therapy to regain his normal gait.

Nita Edwards was scientifically documented as completely paralyzed for a year. Her normal gait returned on Friday, February 11, 1977, at 3:30 p.m., Sri Lanka time, the very moment of her healing.

A few years after this healing, my husband and I had the pleasure of getting to know Nita. We found her to be a radiant Christian with a deep desire for God to be glorified through her life and testimony. He has been fulfilling that desire in many different ways.

Miracles of Healing

For some reason, we are apt to think that miraculous healings of the mind are less likely to take place than miraculous healings related to other parts of the body. Perhaps that concept comes from having heard of fewer medically-proven cases. That's why I have chosen the following story:

Barbara (the name has been changed) received the Lord Jesus Christ as her Savior in 1967 and attended regular Bible studies. But three years later found her increasingly involved in her career, with less time given to the reading of God's Word...eventually giving it up altogether. She gradually drifted away from the Lord and His people.

During the next 20 years, although she gained national recognition as a successful career person, she was a dismal failure spiritually.

In the early part of 1983, she began to have memory problems. At first they seemed minor, something to joke about...but progressively, the forgetfulness had a negative impact on her work. She would call her staff to strategy planning meetings to present long- and short-term plans, then discover part way through that an important segment was missing.

Another example was that she would lay out feasibility studies, then be unable to find a key part she had spent hours working on. This meant frantically going through files and drawers, not finding it, having to try and explain why, then having to reconstruct the studies again. Or, worse still, she would come across the missing part later in a totally unrelated file!

Her problem escalated when she suddenly found herself unable to remember explicit instructions...discovering her failure when the work was not done or not completed.

One day she arrived at work and couldn't remember the location of her assigned parking spot. She had been using that same spot for the past year, but thereafter, had to carry the instructions in a notebook.

There were times when Barbara couldn't remember how to get back to her home in her car. She would pull over to the side of the road, frantically trying to recognize some familiar landmark. Finding a phone, she would call home, making a joke about being lost and then discover that she was relatively near her house.

She consulted her family doctor, who referred her to a specialist for in-depth testing. The results were that she was in the early stages of Alzheimer's disease.

His prognosis was for Barbara to quit working and relieve the stress-oriented areas of her life, with no hope medically for a cure. She painfully recalled the three months prior to her mother's death, which had been brought on by complications of Alzheimer's.

One morning, after her initial fear had subsided, she was pondering the future when a deep conviction entered into her spirit that this was not the end...that God still had a plan for her life, and that somehow He was going to use these circumstances, and her, for good.

This inner "knowing" that God still had a useful purpose for her life, brought peace and motivated her to get back to reading her Bible on a daily basis.

Each day she prayed, "Dear God, please bring this Book alive to me. Give me understanding as I read. Show me what You want me to do." It was at this point she made Jesus Christ the *Lord* of her life, not just her Savior. Barbara surrendered her will to Him.

This meant that the purpose of reading God's Word was to hear His voice personally so that she could obey what He said. Now that's when Bible reading really became exciting!

It is very interesting to note that Barbara never asked God to heal her...she never even thought about that possibility. She just kept asking God to tell her what to do in order to fulfill His purpose for her life, and believed that He would.

One day, while in prayer, the thought came to her that God wanted her to testify to two of her unconverted friends. She was to tell how she had rededicated her life to the Lord Jesus, and state her conviction that He had a purposeful plan for her life, regardless of having Alzheimer's disease.

This was not easy, and she feared their reactions. But Jesus was now Lord, so she obeyed as she met her friends at a restaurant.

The result was that both friends wanted to hear more about the Lord Jesus and the way of salvation, and she spent two hours telling them. Life was getting more exciting and fulfilling.

Around 10:00 that night, Barbara was driving home from the restaurant. As she drove down a lonely road, she suddenly felt the presence of the Lord so powerfully that she had to pull over to the side of the road. She was shaking uncontrollably,

Some of the Ways of God in Healing

and didn't understand what was happening...when she heard the Lord Jesus speak to her.

She says, "I didn't know this could happen. But His voice seemed to be all around me. First, I heard my name, and then He said that He loved me, and was pleased that I had done what He had asked me to do. He then explained that He had to take everything away from me, that I had allowed to crowd Him out of my life. Then He said, 'And now you are healed.'"

In a moment of time, Barbara had instant memory recall of the times during the previous 20 years she had made choices when God had prompted her to go a certain way. Almost always she had gone another way...her way.

God then gave her clear directions as to what she was to do next, and an understanding of what He was going to do with her in the future.

It was about 20 minutes later before she stopped shaking and was able to drive the car home.

About a year later, at the urging of her doctor, she went back to the specialist for a checkup. When she took one of the key short-term memory tests, he found a distinct difference. In fact, the specialist said he had *never* seen a reversal such as in Barbara's case. He asked her if she had any idea how the change had taken place. She simply testified to God's supernatural intervention, which caused the doctor to raise his eyebrows. But he had no other explanation.

Today Barbara is busily involved in the service of the Lord, spending much time counseling needy people. Her effectiveness in ministry is because she has made it a way of life to spend quality time daily alone with the Lord...in prayer and in His Word, and then to be obedient to what He tells her to do.

Disobedience to revealed truth was the cause of her problems. Obedience became the key to her sustained healing and close relationship with God.

11

Miraculous Grace

Another purpose for illness can be to demonstrate that the grace of God is sufficient, even when the person is not healed.

As a child, I observed that it was normal for Dad and Mother to pray for healing. My father's sister had a miraculous healing from cancer. My dad not only believed in divine healing, but as a Bible teacher taught on the subject. And yet he was not healed of Parkinson's disease. Undaunted, he prayed for others and saw them healed.

Did he have understanding as to why God didn't heal him? I don't think so! Did he have an understanding of the character of God, who didn't heal him? Most definitely! I'd say, "Dad, how are you today?" He'd always say, "Fine." Often he would add, "God's grace is sufficient." Sometimes he would comment as Job did, *"Though He slay me, yet will I trust Him..."* (Job 13:15 KJV).

He praised the Lord, and said by his life, "He's faithful. He knows what He's doing with me." There was no resentment toward God. I learned from his life that God's grace was sufficient, and that God's strength was made perfect in his weakness.

This left a deep imprint upon my spirit. It has produced a solid faith in the character of God, even when there's no understanding why much prayer is not answered in the way we would ask or expect.

I not only still believe in God's miraculous healing power, having experienced it numerous times myself, but I have a testimony of what I learned through my father's reaction to God's sovereignty that I wouldn't trade for anything in the world. I never once heard him complain. I never once heard him questioning God's love, or faithfulness or justice.

Divine ability from God to cope in difficult circumstances with praise on our lips, peace of mind and joy in our hearts—that's grace. My dad had it.

The point is this: I believe that the demonstration of the grace of God on my father was every bit as miraculous as any demonstration of the power of God in the most dramatic healings I've ever seen. Both are miracles.

God's words to the apostle Paul about this supernatural grace came after he had pled with the Lord three times to take away "...*a thorn in my flesh, a messenger of Satan, to torment me*" (II Corinthians 12:7).

Instead of healing and deliverance from the problem, in God's infinite wisdom and knowledge He

Miraculous Grace

said, *"...My grace is sufficient for you, for my power is made perfect in weakness..."* (II Corinthians 12:9).

Paul's reaction was a very positive one. He said in effect, "OK, God, I'll buy that! In fact, I'm excited about this weakness now, because You say Your power will be on me in greater measure." This response produced spiritual, mental and emotional health in Paul...and an acceleration of God's eternal purposes for His Church through this same man.

To see the shining faces of those who are physically disabled, who have been denied healing but have no resentment to God, is to see this miraculous grace powerfully at work.

One day my husband and I went to visit a friend. We met his lovely daughter, who was with a young man, his legs totally paralyzed from a football accident. He was in a wheelchair.

The first thing I noticed were his dark brown eyes. They were so soft. His face was radiant, and although I knew nothing about him and was just introduced to him, I walked right over to him, looked into his eyes intently and said, "I love you. I'll tell you one of the reasons I love you. I don't have to ask you one single thing. I see the wheelchair. I see your legs hanging limp, and I see there's not a particle of resentment in your eyes toward God. I don't need to hear your story to know that you have come to terms with God in total rest."

I said, "Your eyes have no questions, there's no hardness in them. You're in love with Jesus. His grace is sufficient. It doesn't matter to you whether you are healed or you're not healed. You're living for the glory of God. Young man, I love you!" Then I heard the story that proved the truth of what I had said. The Holy Spirit had given me that instantaneous witness through the shining countenance of that young man.

He told me he *had* been bitter, he *had* had questions. But he had come to understand as he had pored over the Word of God, and as he looked into the face of Jesus, that God was "...*just in all his ways, and kind in all his doings,*" just as the Bible says in Psalm 145:17 (RSV).

He shared with enthusiasm some of the dynamic purposes that God had started to reveal for his life since he accepted God's sovereignty and received God's miraculous grace. God had shown him that he was to write a book about his life, and this lovely Christian girlfriend was helping him do it.

Physical healing? No. Spiritual, mental and emotional healing? Yes. A manifestation of miraculous grace and powerful purpose.

12

Demonstrating the Mercy of God

Another purpose for illness is to give God an opportunity to demonstrate His mercy. The first purpose was to demonstrate His power, second was to demonstrate His miraculous grace, third to demonstrate His mercy. What is mercy? Not getting what we deserve.

Matthew 15:22 says, "*A Canaanite woman from that vicinity came to him, crying out, 'Lord, Son of David, have mercy on me! My daughter is suffering terribly from demon-possession.'*" The Lord Jesus responded to her cry that was based in humility. In effect, she was saying, "Dear God, would You please meet my need, not because I deserve it. I know I don't, but because of Your mercy."

Katherine Kuhlman said on one occasion, "If I was asked to give the explanation in one word only, of what happens by God's spirit in the demonstrations of all the miraculous in these miracle services, that one word would be mercy; the mercy of God."

My comment is, what else is the explanation of the fact that the large majority of the people, often with the most dramatic healings, were people who rarely, if ever, attended church?

Often people came to her services with cynical minds and hearts devoid of faith, when suddenly the mercy of God was extended to them and they were dramatically healed. They would then come up to the platform and she would say, "How long has it been since you've been to church?" "Haven't been to church in 25 years." They just walked out of a wheel-chair or were healed of cancer or some incurable disease. I heard it time and time again in her services. And she would say, "Oh, the mercy of God!" What for? To bring the people to repentance of sin so that their souls may be saved. This was the bigger miracle.

Romans 2:4 says, *"Or do you show contempt for the riches of his kindness, tolerance and patience, not realizing that God's kindness leads you toward repentance?"* How many of us have been healed by God because it was a demonstration of His mercy? We didn't deserve it. Did we get the message and see that He demonstrated His goodness to us so that we would start shaping up?

Let's look at people in the Bible who cried out to God for mercy and were healed. In Luke 18:35-37, when the blind beggar sitting by the roadside heard that Jesus of Nazareth was passing by, he cried, *"...Jesus, Son of David, have mercy on me!"* (Give me what I don't deserve.) Jesus granted his request.

In Mark 5:19, when the demoniac with the legion of demons was set free, he wanted to remain with

Demonstrating the Mercy of God

Jesus, who said, "...*Go home to your family and tell them how much the Lord has done for you, and how he has had mercy on you.*"

You may not be able to relate to a blind man, a woman with a demon-possessed child or a demoniac. But maybe you can relate to Epaphroditus, one of Paul's close friends. In Philippians 2:26-27 we read, "*For he longs for all of you and is distressed because you heard he was ill. Indeed he was ill, and almost died. But God had mercy on him, and not on him only but also on me, to spare me sorrow upon sorrow.*" The explanation of Epaphroditus finally coming back to health was the release of the mercy of God.

The Bible is so balanced. If only we would read and study it! We may seek God for healing with an attitude of heart that we deserve to be healed, because of all we've done in service for Him and others. God may well hold back that healing.

The Bible teaches us that when we have done all that we should do, we are unprofitable servants (Luke 17:10). The person who prays, "God, I'm an unprofitable servant. I'm not worthy of the least of your favors. But please, have mercy upon me," is far more likely to get God's attention...and the needed healing. Humility makes the difference.

13

A Means of Testing

In order for God to test us, we often need to have some difficult circumstances. Sickness and/or pain can be used by God to achieve that purpose.

It is significant that Paul urges in Romans 12:1 *"...in view of God's mercy, to offer your **bodies** as living sacrifices, holy and pleasing to God—this is your spiritual act of worship."*

We can be sure if we have followed through with that admonition, God will test our sincerity as it relates to our bodies.

It is very important to understand that God's absolute justice and righteousness are behind every test. *"...O Lord Almighty, you who judge righteously and test the heart and mind..."* (Jeremiah 11:20).

God tests us to see whether we really love Him (Deuteronomy 13:3), whether we will obey Him (Deuteronomy 8:2; Judges 2:21-22), and the purity of our motives (I Thessalonians 2:3-4).

Some of the Ways of God in Healing

Test one: We have said, "God, I want to live for Your glory in any way You want." Then suddenly we find ourselves in pain or hurting emotionally. Do we respond by saying we don't want this kind of suffering, we don't want the difficulties? God may well be thinking "Didn't you say you wanted Me to be glorified? Why do you squeal when I create or allow difficult circumstances to bring glory to My name?"

He didn't promise that it would always be easy for us. In fact, suffering is an inevitable part of helping our spiritual growth, if we respond to God correctly. *"And the God of all grace, who called you to his eternal glory in Christ, after you have suffered a little while, will himself restore you and make you strong, firm and steadfast"* (I Peter 5:10).

Many years ago, when I lived in New Zealand, I was driving my car, when severe pain suddenly gripped the back of my neck. I immediately took authority over the powers of darkness, but the pain continued. So I knew it wasn't the enemy.

I said, "Oh well, God, I have told You that I want to live for Your glory any way that You should choose. So if You want me to spend the rest of my life with this severe pain in my neck, and by doing so You can bring more glory to Your name, then that's OK with me." And I meant it with all my heart. I had no release whatsoever to pray for healing. I drove on, and then noticed that the pain had gone. I understood that this was a test from God, given, received and passed by His grace.

Test two: To see whether we will go on being obedient to what God has told us to do, regardless of how we feel.

Jim and I were flying home to Los Angeles via Dallas, Texas. The plane descended too rapidly, and as a result, I went almost deaf in my left ear. During the two hours at the Dallas airport, pain developed in the same ear. It became so intense on the remainder of the flight that on arrival in Los Angeles, Jim took me immediately to a doctor near the airport.

The Holy Spirit spoke the words "Psalm 142 verse three" into Jim's mind as he sought God on my behalf. He couldn't remember what those verses were, but on looking them up, found they were exactly what I needed to hear. *"When my spirit grows faint within me, it is you who know my way...."* I was assured and comforted.

The doctor's diagnosis: a bend in the ear, nose and throat canal. He explained that sometimes airline pilots experience this, and he knew that it was extremely painful. He said he couldn't give me anything to help, but that in time the pain would subside.

After two hours of driving in dense Los Angeles traffic, we arrived home. Nine and a half long hours after the pain started, I finally got relief.

In my devotional Scripture reading the next morning, God gave me some of the understanding for which I had been asking. *"The righteous cry out, and the Lord hears them; he delivers them from all their troubles....A righteous man may have many troubles, but the Lord delivers him from them all"* (Psalm 34:17,19).

Afflictions are part of God's discipleship course for His children, but they don't last forever. There is a point of deliverance. Second Peter 2:9 (RSV) says the same thing. *"...the Lord knows how to rescue the godly from trial...."*

The doctor had cautioned me that the worst thing I could do would be to go up in another plane—for some considerable time—as my problem was caused by sudden changes in air pressure.

I was due to leave for ministry in Europe in eleven days. I would be away for three and a half weeks, and would be on a number of planes. What was I to do in the light of the doctor's warning?

The issue was quickly settled in my mind and heart. Go right on with the plans God had revealed to me, regardless of the consequences.

I have never experienced ear trouble since, and have been flying frequently on the King's business. Unconditional obedience is the only kind of obedience that impresses God.

A week later, while in Germany, I developed severe pain across my lower back. It felt like hot knives were stabbing me. I could only walk with a stoop. I wondered how I would make it through, as I walked to the podium to speak at the first meeting.

As soon as I opened my mouth to speak, all pain instantly left me. I thought I was healed. But when I walked off the platform, the pain returned in full force.

In response to my praying the four key prayers in Chapter Three of this book, God spoke to me from Psalm 11:4-5, explaining that He was testing me. From Psalm 9:8-10 He reiterated His justice to me, and that He was my stronghold in times of trouble. He also assured me that He never forsakes those who seek Him, nor does He ignore the cry of the afflicted.

I was also reminded that I needed to keep praising Him. I did.

That whole night I sat up on a sofa in our hotel room, propped up with pillows. It was too painful to lie down. Amazingly, I slept.

The next morning, the Lord directed Jim to the book of Job, with the understanding that God had allowed the enemy to afflict me over recent weeks in order for God to test me. At the same time, the Holy Spirit greatly encouraged and comforted me from my devotional reading in Psalm 71. I also noticed five references to praising God in that psalm, and realized that as I continued to worship, praise and trust Him during these afflictions, I could claim the resultant promises in verses 20 and 21. *"Though you have made me see troubles, many and bitter, you will restore my life again....You will increase my honor and comfort me once again."*

By the middle of the afternoon, I was completely healed. The purposes for God having tested me were passed by His grace.

But I was yet to hear a surprising sequel to this experience. At the meeting that evening, a German-speaking American lady told me that she had been awakened by the Lord the previous night. She was in the same hotel as we were, only a few doors away.

She received a clear impression to her mind, "Pray for Joy. She needs healing." Her immediate response was, "Joy who?" "The lady who gave the message at the opening meeting of the conference tonight." She thought it strange to be asked to sacrifice sleep time for a person she had only spoken to briefly that night, and really didn't know anything about.

However, she prayed for my healing, and tried to sleep again. But the Lord wouldn't let her. He impressed a strong burden on her spirit, which resulted in her prevailing before God at some length, with the understanding that the disorder was in the trunk of my body. Finally she was released to go back to sleep.

She asked me the next day if any of what she had been through made any sense to me, as I had appeared to be in good health when I was giving the message the previous night. I told her my story, and we marvelled together at some of the ways of God in healing.

These stories highlight the wonderfully kind and caring character of our Heavenly Father—even though He permitted the enemy to afflict me as a means of testing.

We can never take any credit for passing tests. It's all a result of God's Spirit who teaches us His ways. It's His grace that enables us. So the glory is *all His* (Romans 11:36).

Test three: Whether we will obey God as in Philippians 4:4, "*Rejoice in the Lord always. I will say it again: Rejoice!*" Regardless of circumstances.

I was asked to pray for a man at a summer convention who had three huge boils on the back of his neck. He was in a lot of pain. I sought God for directions. God said to me, "Get him to ask Me what it is I'm trying to teach him. That's all I want you to say." So I did, and left him with the assurance that I would pray that he would hear God clearly.

A few days later, he sent for me again and said, "I didn't like it when all you did was say, 'Ask God to show you what He wants to teach you,' but was it ever right! When I sought God diligently for that answer, He said to me, 'Bob, you've always praised Me when everything's going great and I'm thrilled to have your praises, but you have never learned to praise Me through suffering.' 'Oh, that's right, God. OK, so this is what You're trying to teach me.'"

Then he said, "Joy, I noticed that from the moment I started to praise God for who He is, regardless of the circumstances or the pain, and maintained that praise, I started to get relief from pain, and the boils started to heal. I wouldn't have missed this learning time for anything. Thank you for your obedience to God on my behalf."

Test four: Whether we will keep worshiping God with a trusting heart in the midst of great trial, or get bitter and resist Him.

The life of Job is a graphic illustration. It includes satanic attack, tests passed, much physical suffering, tests failed, humbling and then healing.

The Word of God clearly shows us in this saga of human suffering that God took the initiative in bringing Job to Satan's attention. God then proceeded to give him a very impressive description of Job's character, "...*There is no one on earth like him; he is blameless and upright, a man who fears God and shuns evil*" (Job 1:8). Quite a commercial, when you consider it came from God!

Satan immediately challenged God about Job's motives. He said that Job's righteous life was a result of all the blessings God had showered upon him.

Some of the Ways of God in Healing

And if that was reversed, Job would curse God to His face—quite a statement!

God then gave Satan permission to do what he wanted with everything Job had, but not to touch Job himself. As a result, Job lost all his possessions and all his children in one day. His magnificent response was to worship God and praise Him for His unquestionable sovereignty. So far, so good!

After God had challenged Satan with Job's reaction, Satan said in effect, "If You allow me permission to bring suffering in his body, I'll prove to You that he'll curse You to Your face."

In order for God to test the most righteous man in all the earth, He allowed Satan to put painful sores all over Job's body...*but not to take his life.*

This tells us that we are not puppets on the end of Satan's strings. As we walk in obedience to God and live holy lives, God will only allow satanic forces to attack us in order to teach us something and ultimately to do us good. We find that out through seeking God for understanding.

That's where Job seemed to miss it. There is little evidence after Job Chapter Three, of Job asking God what He was trying to teach him. As a result, he never received the understanding God would have undoubtedly given him. That is, he was being tested by God in his body, and a satanic attack was part of the test.

Job concluded that God was angry with him, and deeply resented what he considered was unjust treatment. He repeatedly tried to justify this attitude.

The following Scriptures are a few of many that make that clear.

"If I summoned him and he answered me, I would not believe that he was listening to my voice. For he crushes me with a tempest and multiplies my wounds without cause; he will not let me get my breath, but fills me with bitterness" (Job 9:16-18 RSV).

"...though I am blameless, He would prove me perverse" (verse 20).

"...As surely as God lives, who has denied me justice, the Almighty, who has made me taste bitterness of soul..." (Job 27:2).

Also, Job 30:21-22.

In the midst of all this, Job makes some classic statements of faith and trust in God.

"I know that my Redeemer lives, and that in the end he will stand upon the earth. And after my skin has been destroyed, yet in my flesh I will see God" (Job 19:25-26).

"Though He slay me, yet will I trust Him..." (Job 13:15 NKJV).

"But he knows the way that I take; when he has tested me, I will come forth as gold" (Job 23:10).

It's easy for many to identify with Job in his mixed reactions. Sometimes we're trusting in God's character, and other times we're wondering if God has forgotten our address!

We may not curse God to His face, but our lack of worship, praise and obedience, coupled with our murmuring, sends out the signals that we're not pleased with God's treatment of us.

We can be righteous before God, as Job was, *before* God tests us, but we can become unrighteous by our reactions to Him (and others) during testing. This can prolong the suffering, because we then start reaping the consequences of our sinful sowing.

When we are grounded in the knowledge of God's absolute justice, it is unthinkable and unreasonable to attach blame to Him, even though He may have caused or allowed the circumstances.

He not only *is* just, but He loves justice. *"The Lord loves righteousness and justice; the earth is full of His unfailing love"* (Psalm 33:5).

After God gave Job a fresh revelation of His unparalleled greatness, limitless power and infinite knowledge, Job repented of having accused God of doing wrong. He admitted to God that previously he had only a limited knowledge of His character (Job 42:5-6).

Job had to pray for his friends who had misjudged him, and then healing was granted to him. God is always working for our good through times of testing. When the tests are passed, God rewards us. He gave Job twice as much as He had allowed the enemy to take from him.

If we fail to pass the tests, God has to create or allow more difficult circumstances, hoping we will get the message, receive His grace, and walk in obedience to His ways from His Word.

The rewards of passing tests are a more intimate relationship with God and greater privileges and responsibilities related to His kingdom.

For a more comprehensive coverage of the subject of "The Testing of God's Children," I have a series of three taped messages, which explain how to recognize tests from God, and the biblical way to react.

A Means of Testing

Another taped message, "The Ways of God in Testing," gives understanding about how God manifests His character to His children when they are going through trials.

These messages are available from Pilgrim Tapes. Their address is at the back of the book.

14

Don't Presume

As we diligently seek God for understanding of what He wants to teach us through pain, at times He reveals that there is a combination of the things into which we have already looked.

It was after many years of pursuing the understanding of the ways of God that I discovered this truth.

For a number of days I had pain in my body. I had done spiritual warfare and prayed the four prayers outlined in Chapter Three. God started to answer by convicting me of something that was displeasing to Him. I sincerely repented and humbled myself before God. I also shared this with my husband.

The debilitating pain continued, and my persistent inquiries to God for further understanding brought no answers. I had no witness in my spirit, or direction from the Lord to go to a doctor, although I was very open to doing so.

I realized the responsibility was upon God to tell me the next thing I was to do, in response to the fourth prayer in Chapter Three. I awoke one morning with the impression that I was to ask Jim to seek the Lord on my behalf for any understanding of what God was trying to teach me or explain to me.

When Jim did so, God directed him to Zechariah 13:9, with the clear understanding that God was using the pain as a means of testing me. *"This third I will bring into the fire; I will refine them like silver and test them like gold. They will call on my name and I will answer them; I will say, 'They are my people,' and they will say, 'The Lord is our God.'"*

I embraced this revelation by praising God and thanking Him for answering me through my precious husband. As I received God's grace to cope with the physical discomfort and restricted mobility, and maintained an attitude of worship, the pain gradually subsided.

I learned that the causes of sickness and the purposes of sickness can be combined, and I'll only know when they are, through diligently seeking God for understanding.

On another occasion, I was in physical discomfort and God used it to get my attention about something for which I needed to repent. As soon as I had done so, He spoke very clearly to me from Daniel 11:33-35, *"Those who are wise will instruct many....Some of the wise will stumble, so that they may be refined, purified and made spotless until the time of the end...."*

I experienced the combination of being rebuked by the Lord and then not only receiving real encouragement from Him, but a speedy healing.

Don't Presume

We also need to understand that even when sin has been the cause of our suffering, and our repentance has released God's forgiveness, we may not always receive healing immediately. The law of reaping may still be operative in our lives.

This reminder in our bodies helps to prevent us from sinning in the same way again.

Knowing this will keep us from wrongly presuming that God doesn't love us or has not forgiven us.

The amount of reaping time we experience is according to:

- The depth of our repentance.

- The extent of our willingness to humble ourselves and make any restitution God should require of us.

- Our asking God for His mercy to be extended toward us.

- Others interceding for mercy on our behalf.

15

Humbling Ourselves Releases God's Healing Power

During a time of teaching at a Youth With A Mission School of Evangelism in Switzerland in 1971, the above truth was dramatically illustrated in my life.

One afternoon between teaching sessions, I suddenly developed severe pain in my stomach and felt ill enough to know I needed to call for help. Two of the staff were trained nurses, and upon taking one look at me, were convinced that something was seriously wrong. Their diagnosis was food poisoning, although we were at a loss to know what could have caused it.

The pain was so severe that my breathing was coming in short gasps, and my voice was reduced to a whisper. I heard them say, "We will have to get a stomach pump to work on her."

At that point, I indicated that first I needed to ask God if there was any undealt-with sin in my life. I was not aware of any. They understood the spiritual principle of seeking God, and waited while I silently prayed.

Immediately God convicted me of the sin of pride, and He pinpointed it. That morning I had received two letters that related to my ministry, from spiritual leaders in different nations, and I had become impressed that they had written to me. I had become impressed with *myself*. God let me know that He was totally unimpressed! I quickly repented of the pride, and knew I was forgiven, but the pain remained.

I then became aware that I needed to humble myself before my friends and tell them exactly what God had shown me. I did so immediately, and just as suddenly, the pain subsided and then stopped.

Much to the relief of the two nurses, they saw my face turn from ashen grey to white.

Within seven minutes I was on my feet, a little weak and shaken, but declaring that there was absolutely no need for any more concern about my physical condition. God had revealed the cause and purpose for the illness, and in His mercy had released His power through repentance and humbling. Praise His wonderful name!

You may wonder at the severity of God's dealings with me. But there are several things we need to keep in perspective.

First, the truth that God is always absolutely just. *"He is the Rock, his works are perfect, and all his ways are just. A faithful God who does no wrong, upright and just is he"* (Deuteronomy 32:4).

Second, that pride is obnoxious to God. "...*I hate pride and arrogance...*" (Proverbs 8:13).

Third, that those who teach God's Word will be judged with greater strictness if they do not live according to its standards. "*Not many of you should presume to be teachers, my brothers, because you know that we who teach will be judged more strictly*" (James 3:1).

In James 5:14-16, we find that there are a number of things involved with the releasing of God's healing power.

> The first is for the sick person to call the elders of the church.
>
> The second is to ask them to pray in the name of the Lord.
>
> The third is for the elders to anoint the sick person with oil.
>
> The fourth is that they must pray in faith.
>
> The fifth is that sins need to be dealt with by confessing them to one another, and then praying for one another.

Then God promises to forgive the sins, heal the sickness and restore the person to health.

It is often so much easier to fulfill the first four conditions and hope that God will release His power, than to humble ourselves and fulfill all the conditions. But God knows that our deadliest sin is the sin of pride, and He knows our desperate need to be delivered from it. Humbling ourselves is therefore the way of release and freedom.

A friend of ours was directed by God to spend a number of days in prayer and fasting while staying in our home. At the end of the fast, he asked us to pray for the healing of his back and stomach. When we sought God, He clearly confirmed to us through His Word that this was what we were to do.

My husband and I laid our hands upon our friend's shoulders while he sat in a chair, in readiness for God to direct us in prayer. I was puzzled and felt embarrassed, because there was no release in my spirit to pray one word, and no direction given to me after minutes of silence.

Upon inquiring of the Lord for understanding, I repeatedly received the impression to my mind of "James 5:16." Being familiar with the verse, I realized that God was speaking about the need for sins to be confessed to one another prior to the prayer of faith for healing. I was aware that could mean my sins, and invited God to convict me.

When no conviction came and the impression remained, I realized I would have to explain why I still had no release to pray. I did so, although I found it very difficult. I cringed at the thought of our dear friend having to humble himself before us.

His response was immediate. He shared that during the time of fasting, God had convicted him of a number of sins. He had said to God, "If you want me to confess them openly, then confirm it in some way through Jim or Joy."

As soon as he did, we were immediately released to pray the prayer of faith. God, in His mercy and faithfulness, released His healing power. *As for God, his way is perfect; the word of the Lord is flawless* (Psalm 18:30).

The story of Naaman's healing from leprosy in II Kings 5 also vividly illustrates the connection between humbling and healing.

It would be humiliating for the general of the Assyrian army to arrive at Elisha's door with his horses and chariots and entourage, then have to receive the prescription for the cure of his leprosy from a servant...not even an interview with the prophet! And worse still, to be told that he would have to wash himself seven times in the Jordan River, when the rivers in his own land were far superior. Why *that* river? Why seven times? What would people think? He would look and feel foolish.

The Bible says he was offended and angry...until his servants encouraged him to take the simple, humbling steps of obedience to the word of the Lord. God's healing power was then released.

Humbling before healing is not only what God often requires on a personal basis, but it is significant that it is the first condition in II Chronicles 7:14 for the healing of a nation.

"If My people, who are called by my name, will humble themselves and pray and seek my face and turn from their wicked ways, then will I hear from heaven and will forgive their sin and will heal their land."

God is not impressed with prayers that come from proud hearts. According to James 5:16, it is the prayer of a *righteous* man that is powerful and effective. And we're only as righteous as we are humble.

Perhaps we've been puzzled why our many prayers for healing have gone unanswered. Confessing our sins to one another could be the means of releasing God's mighty power. In His faithfulness, He will direct us to the right person.

16

A Time to Die

This is an interesting point, and must be realistically faced as we study the subject of some of the ways of God in healing.

The plain fact is that perhaps God may be glorified more by our death than by our life...or by the death of someone near and dear to us.

When we are truly living for the glory of God, it will not be a matter of concern to us *how* God is glorified through us or our loved ones...just as long as He is! We can only totally relinquish ourselves and others to God when we are grounded in the revelation of God's character...His infinite wisdom and knowledge, His absolute justice, His unswerving faithfulness, His matchless grace and His unfathomable love.

Paul had this knowledge of God. That's why he said, *"I eagerly expect and hope that I will in no way be ashamed, but will have sufficient courage so that now as always Christ will be exalted in my body, whether by life*

Some of the Ways of God in Healing

or by death. For to me, to live is Christ and to die is gain" (Philippians 1:20-21).

For many years, my husband and I had the great privilege, pleasure and blessing of having a very close relationship with an older woman here in the United States who loved us like a mother. And we heartily reciprocated that love.

As she was a godly, dedicated soul with a great love for the Lord, as well as being a real intercessor, we were very puzzled as to why she was so often ill. She was also a woman of great faith in God.

It was at a time of physical crisis, after she returned home from yet another period of hospitalization, that I asked her directly if she had ever relinquished to the Lord her right to live.

To my amazement, she said, "No." She made it quite clear that she was not willing to die. It was only after I gently but firmly counseled her, that she finally realized she had not made Jesus "Lord" as it related to her death. After a struggle, she finally surrendered this part of her will to the One she had loved and faithfully served for a lifetime. Some months later, she died.

It was a point of discovery to Jim and me that one of the saintliest people, in our estimation, had spent a lifetime not being willing for God to be more glorified by her death than by her life.

Elisha's life is an example of "It's time to die." In II Kings 13:14 we read *"Now when Elisha [the prophet] had fallen sick with the illness of which he was to die, Joash king of Israel went down to him..."* (RSV).

What does that tell us? The purpose in that sickness was death. It would have been pointless to have said to Elisha at this time in his life, "Now we need to fast and pray over you and have a healing service and anoint you with oil." That would have been a waste of time.

We need to ask God for understanding of the purpose for the sickness. If He reveals that it is death, then we need to pray for divine grace to be upon us or the dying person, and that all God's purposes will be accomplished in them and through them until the time of their death.

My precious mother died of cancer a few weeks before her 87th birthday. I have never seen anyone more ready to die, or longing to be with the Lord she loved, or more at peace through months of terminal illness.

She had believed in, and personally experienced divine healing throughout her life, but when it was "a time to die," she knew it and totally embraced it as a loving provision from the Lord. She exuded the "peace that passes understanding" and as such, was a great testimony to God's grace and her name, Grace.

I heard her say many times as I was growing up, "There are thousands of experiences worse than death, or facing death. Heaven is a wonderful place." A number of times she said, "Ever since I was converted at the age of twelve, I have longed to be with the Lord Jesus." What a heritage is mine!

It's not surprising, therefore, that my definition of death is "seeing Jesus a little sooner than others."

In Ecclesiastes 3:1-2 Solomon says, *"There is a time for everything, and a season for every activity under heaven: a time to be born and a time to die...."*

Let's ask God to so prepare us for *His time* for us to die that we will embrace it as His loving provision for us, and glorify Him by our death.

*"He has made everything beautiful **in its time**..."* (Ecclesiastes 3:11).

Perhaps we thought we had every indication from God, to believe that He was going to heal a person for whom we had prayed. It came as a shock when the person died. This is not an uncommon experience.

We can react with a resentful cry of, "Why, God?" Or we can rest in the certainty of the perfection of God's character and the inscrutability of His ways, being assured He has answered our prayers for their healing in a better way.

For our unanswered questions, we can take comfort in Jesus' words, *"You do not realize now what I am doing, but later you will understand"* (John 13:7).

When a loved one has died, God understands the pain of our grief-stricken hearts. *"...his understanding no one can fathom"* (Isaiah 40:28). *"...he is mighty in strength of understanding"* (Job 36:5 RSV).

He also knows that we need an emotional healing. I know of no better promise to lay hold on in faith, than, *"He heals the brokenhearted and binds up their wounds"* (Psalm 147:3).

Faith in God's Word will, in time, bring the results. *"He sent forth his word and healed them"* (Psalm 107:20).

17

Death and Resurrection

Perhaps God wants to be glorified through a death and resurrection, as in the case of Lazarus in John 11. Mary and Martha didn't want it that way. They wanted Lazarus to be healed, and thought Jesus had missed it by not coming sooner to their dying brother.

They had to learn what we have to learn...and experience is a wonderful teacher. *"'For my thoughts are not your thoughts, neither are your ways my ways,' declares the Lord. 'As the heavens are higher than the earth, so are my ways higher than your ways and my thoughts than your thoughts'"* (Isaiah 55:8-9).

The following story illustrates this powerfully.

In June 1985, a six-year-old boy from Kinshasa, Zaire, Africa, developed a high fever with a temperature of 105°F, and became very seriously ill. Upon examination by a doctor, his Christian parents were told that their son Katshini had cerebral malaria. By early Wednesday morning, the child grew worse, so the parents took him to a neighboring clinic.

In the words of Mulamba (Katshini's father), "As we approached Mikondo Clinic, Katshini suddenly arched his body and threw back his head. He had a discharge from his bowels and stopped breathing. My son had died in my arms!"

It was about 4:00 in the morning. After two attempts to revive the boy with injections had failed, the doctor said, "I can't do anything more to help you. Your child is dead."

Mulamba was sent to the Mama Yemo Hospital from the clinic to obtain a certificate to bury the child. When they arrived at the hospital, they were asked for money to pay for the certificate, but they did not have enough. Mulamba went to the company he worked for to borrow some money.

At that point, Mulamba prayed a very significant prayer, the prayer of relinquishment. "You are the great God. If it brings You glory for Katshini to remain dead, then let it be. But if not, then let him live again." He recalled how Dorcas had been brought back from the dead when Peter prayed for her (Acts 9:36-42).

He also thought about an evangelist from America, Mahesh Chavda, who was having evangelistic meetings in his city. He remembered hearing the testimonies of many who had been healed when Mahesh had prayed for them.

Faith entered into his heart that if Mahesh would pray for his son, God would bring the boy back to life.

Death and Resurrection

By the time he arrived at the meeting, it was noon and the preaching had stopped. But then an amazing thing happened. The evangelist came back to the microphone and said, "God has just shown me that there is a man here whose son has died this morning. God wants you to be sure that He is going to raise your son from the dead today. If that man can hear my voice, let him come to the platform and we will pray."

Mulamba pushed his way through the crowd and identified himself, explaining that he had left his dead son at the hospital and that he was seeking God's help. Mulamba says, "Mahesh Chavda laid his hands on me and prayed a simple prayer. He bound the powers of darkness and death in the name of Jesus Christ. Then he loosed the spirit of resurrection to restore Katshini's life. I was positive God had heard the prayer and was answering.

"When I went quickly back to the hospital where I had left my family, I heard the most wonderful sound of my life. It was Katshini's voice, and he was calling for me! I hurried inside and took him in my arms. As a family we greatly rejoiced together in the Lord! God had given up His firstborn Son to death and now by Him, God had given my firstborn son back to me alive!"

Mulamba's brother, who was not a Christian, had witnessed all these events, and as a direct result committed his life to Christ.

The testimony of this resurrected child has been confirmed by other witnesses, including medical personnel, local pastors and family members.

Some of the Ways of God in Healing

It powerfully illustrates again the truths from Deuteronomy 32:39, *"See now that I myself am He! There is no god besides me. I put to death and I bring to life, I have wounded and I will heal, and no one can deliver out of my hand."*

18

Obedience Again the Key

God is just as glorified by a gradual healing, whether solely through prayer or through prayer plus medical means.

Let's look at the Word of God in Mark 8:23-25, *"He [Jesus] took the blind man by the hand and led him outside the village. When he had spit on the man's eyes and put his hands on him, Jesus asked, 'Do you see anything?' He looked up and said, 'I see people; they look like trees walking around.' Once more Jesus put his hands on the man's eyes. Then his eyes were opened, his sight was restored, and he saw everything clearly."* This was obviously a gradual healing.

Was there any failure when Jesus laid hands on the blind man and he wasn't healed the first time? Of course not! Jesus was doing everything the Father was telling Him to do, because that's how He lived.

"Jesus gave them this answer: 'I tell you the truth, the Son can do nothing by himself; he can do only what he

sees his Father doing, because whatever the Father does the Son also does'" (John 5:19).

So why did God the Father temporarily cause a partial healing through Jesus at that time? To teach us that *obedience* is the key, and that we shouldn't give up, but continue to seek God for directions as to the next step. We mustn't presume that we didn't have enough faith. We mustn't judge others. God may well be wanting to tell us to have more prayer, or to come to Him again on behalf of ourselves or others. There will be no confusion if we'll stop, wait, get His orders and then obey.

It gets more interesting as we go on to the next illustration in John chapter 9. We find Jesus with another blind man in a healing process, and this time Jesus is using dirt and spittle. Previously, Jesus just spat on the blind man's eyes. This time, Father God, who told Jesus to do everything, says, "I want You to get some clay and mix it with Your spittle and put it on his eyes."

Let's think about this. Do you think there are medicinal properties in spittle and dirt to make blind eyes see? I don't think so. Therefore, what is the point? Obedience. That's what brought the healing. It was *gradual*, and there were several points of obedience. What did Jesus have to do? Spit, mix it with clay and put it on the man's eyes. Then the man had to go to the Pool of Siloam and wash it off. Do blind eyes see because we wash off spittle and clay in a specific pool? No! But the details had to do with obedience, whether it's one step or many.

We are not to be impressed with the means or the methods of healing, only obedience to the Master.

He has promised in John 10:3-4, "...*the sheep hear his voice, and he calls his own sheep by name and leads them out. When he has brought out all his own, he goes before them, and the sheep follow him, for they know his voice*" (RSV).

"*My sheep hear my voice, and I know them, and they follow me*" (Verse 27, RSV).

"*In your unfailing love you will lead the people you have redeemed. In your strength you will guide them to your holy dwelling*" (Exodus 15:13).

"...*I will lead them beside streams of water on a level path where they will not stumble, because I am Israel's father...*" (Jeremiah 31:9).

In II Kings 20, after the death sentence had been passed on King Hezekiah by God through Isaiah the prophet, Hezekiah wept and prayed. Then God told the prophet to say that He would add fifteen years to his life. "*Then Isaiah said, 'Prepare a poultice of figs.' They did so and applied it to the boil, and he recovered*" (Verse 7).

Do you think that there is any medicinal value in figs for the healing of boils? Maybe; I don't know enough about medical things, but I hardly think that's the point of this story. The significance was in the act of obedience.

It is also important to note that in the account of this same story in Isaiah 38 there is an additional significant factor related to Hezekiah's healing that is not mentioned in either II Kings 20 or II Chronicles 32.

In Isaiah 38:9-20, we have "*a writing of Hezekiah...after his illness and recovery.*" One of God's purposes in Hezekiah's time of illness was to produce a greater degree of humility in this man, who was so greatly used of God in bringing *others* to repentance. *"But what can I say? He has spoken to me, and he himself has done this. I will walk humbly all my years because of this anguish of my soul."*

He goes on to say that the suffering and the humbling were for his benefit, and that his sins had to be recognized and dealt with before God could release His healing power. *"...In your love you kept me from the pit of destruction; you have put all my sins behind your back."*

I was in Japan teaching on the subject of this book to some Youth With A Mission workers who had come from around the world for an evangelistic outreach. After I had stressed the importance of obedience, I said spontaneously, "If God tells you to put a banana on someone's head and then pray for his or her healing, there will be no healing until you obey." They all laughed and I continued on with the message.

At the close, I invited those who needed healing and were prepared to fulfill the conditions of the message, to indicate that, by raising their hands. The first response came from a young woman. The top of one of her feet was severely swollen, and she couldn't even wear an open sandal.

After I had prayed a prayer of faith and had laid my hands on her foot, I straightened up to find a young man, looking awkward and standing behind the girl.

He explained to the whole group that the day before, when he was praying in the prayer room with this girl, he noticed her swollen foot and asked her if he could pray for her healing. When she consented, he had the impression come to his mind, "Pick up that banana and put it on her head." Bananas were among various items of lunch food that were in the prayer room that day. Three times the impression came, but he resisted it. He prayed for her foot, but there was no healing.

He said that as soon as I spoke out the sentence, "If God tells you to put a banana on someone's head, and then pray for his or her healing, there will be no healing until you obey," he knew God was convicting him of disobedience. He repented and thought that was the end of it...until he saw me go and pray for the girl's foot.

God then made it very clear to him that his repentance was to be proved by getting that banana and putting it on her head. He raced up two flights of stairs to the prayer room, got the banana, which amazingly was still there, and had put it on her head while I was bending down and thanking God in faith for His healing power. I didn't see him do this, but the group did. I just heard them repressing their mirth.

Within minutes, her swollen foot was remarkably improved. She was able to continue with the outreach program, which involved much walking in several cities of Japan during the next three weeks. An amused group of about 400 people had an unusual demonstration of signs following the preaching of the Word of God that day.

In order to ensure accuracy in the details of this story, I wrote to the young man who was involved. He shared with me that the main lesson to him was not to be concerned with what people think about our actions (the fear of man) but to be very concerned with what God thinks (the fear of the Lord).

He went on to say that instead of his being humble before the small group in the prayer room, he was humbled (by God) before the larger group of over 400. But he was a good learner, and has been much used of God in full-time missionary and church work for many years.

The Bible teaches us that our love for God is measured by obedience, and that glory can only come to Him through it. Jesus modeled that principle for us. *"I have brought you glory on earth by completing the work you gave me to do"* (John 17:4).

If after seeking God He directs us to go to a doctor to get help, or to a hospital to have treatment or surgery, then that is the way He is going to be glorified. Doctors and nurses are part of God's merciful loving provision to benefit mankind. How I thank God for them. Luke played a very significant role in the Early Church. Isn't it interesting that God chose a medical doctor to write the book of the Acts of the Apostles?

All the knowledge that has been released to medical science for the alleviation of human suffering, and to restore health and maintain it, has come from God.

That's why it is so important to look to the Lord and depend on Him to release His healing power in our bodies, even when He directs us to take medicine or have surgery. Our faith must be in *Him*.

In the last few years, I have heard the testimonies of two senior pastors, two wives of senior pastors, and a young mother of three children, and all have had remarkable healings from terminal cancer.

In each case, God responded to much fervent prayer from many people, as He used doctors and nurses and surgical and medical means to bring them back to full health. Each person has publicly given all the glory to the Lord.

In II Chronicles 16:12 we read about King Asa, "*In the thirty-ninth year of his reign Asa was afflicted with a disease in his feet. Though his disease was severe, even in his illness he did not seek help from the Lord, but only from the physicians.*" His mistake was not that he sought help from doctors, but that he didn't first seek the Lord.

As a young mother, I was in the process of learning the ways of God from His Word. As a result, God gave me plenty of opportunities to apply this message when my children became sick.

For as many times as God would direct me to pray for their healing, and believe Him to do it without any medical means, just as many times He would clearly tell me to pursue medical help.

When our son John was about eight years of age, he had fallen and skinned a large area below his knee. It was badly infected, and resisted all normal treatment.

My husband and I were directed by God to pray that He would supernaturally touch that leg. Before our eyes, instantly, we saw new skin begin to form across that area, all pain left, and the healing process accelerated dramatically. We were in awe of God.

During one very cold and rainy winter during John's childhood, he became sick. Jim was away, and

Some of the Ways of God in Healing

I prayed repeatedly for John's healing. I was hoping that I wouldn't have to take him to a doctor, because my circumstances made that difficult.

I hadn't sought God for direction, presuming that He would heal John in the way that would make it easier for me.

When John got worse after being sick for several days, I knew God was urging me to take him to our doctor. I did, only to be rebuked by him for not having brought John sooner.

I was humbled and repentant before God and my child, asking forgiveness from them both. As soon as John took the prescribed medicine, he started to get well.

God was teaching me that He was willing and able to answer my prayers for my children's healing, but I had to line up with His methods, His means and His ways.

We taught our children the ways of God in healing, and found them very responsive, even if it meant their confessing sin before the healing came. They heard our confessions, too. If we live the truth consistently before our children, they will not find it hard to follow.

How much time and money would be saved, and confusion and even rebellion to God would be avoided, if we would take the time to pray those four important prayers and seek God's face, believing Him to answer, when we are not well?

As a final reminder, the four prayers are:

- I worship You and praise You for the wonder of who You are, and ask that You do something to bring the maximum glory to Your name.

- What are You trying to teach me?
- What are the causes and/or the purposes?
- What is the next thing You want me to do?

Listen to God's incredible encouragement to those who fulfill His conditions:

> *Yet the Lord longs to be gracious to you; he rises to show you compassion. For the Lord is a God of justice. Blessed are all who wait for him! O people of Zion, ...you will weep no more. How gracious he will be when you cry for help! As soon as he hears, he will answer you. Although the Lord gives you the bread of adversity and the water of affliction, your teachers will be hidden no more; with your own eyes you will see them. Whether you turn to the right or to the left, your ears will hear a voice behind you, saying, "This is the way; walk in it"* (Isaiah 30:18-21).

> *He did not say anything to them [the crowds] without using a parable. But when he was alone with his own disciples, He explained everything* (Mark 4:34).

Diligent-seeker-disciples qualify for explanations.

> *The moon will shine like the sun, and the sunlight will be seven times brighter, like the light of seven full days, when the Lord binds up the bruises of his people and heals the wounds he inflicted* (Isaiah 30:26).

The more we want God to be glorified by our lives and in our bodies, and prove it by obedience, the more we will discover that He has planned many ways to lavish His blessings upon us.

Revelation of truth is one of those ways. The explanation of legitimate questions is another.

The closer we are in friendship with others, the more we will trust them with our secrets.

God is the same with His close friends. We choose to obey Him, proving our love for Him. He chooses to reveal some of the secrets of His character and His ways to us from His Word...and that's what this book is really all about.

What a Committal of Life to the Lord Jesus Christ Means

"...Choose you this day whom ye will serve...as for me...[I] will serve the Lord" (Joshua 24:15 KJV).

"From one man he made every nation of men, that they should inhabit the whole earth; and he determined the times set for them and the exact places where they should live. God did this so that men would seek him and perhaps reach out for him and find him, though he is not far from each one of us" (Acts 17:26-27).

1. Acknowledge that you are a sinner and repent of your sin.

"For all have sinned and fall short of the glory of God" (Romans 3:23).

"Repent, then, and turn to God, so that your sins may be wiped out..." (Acts 3:19).

"If we confess our sins, he is faithful and just and will forgive us our sins and purify us from all unrighteousness" (I John 1:9).

2. Believe Christ died and rose again to save you from your sin and to give you eternal life.

"For Christ died for sins once for all, the righteous for the unrighteous, to bring you to God..." (I Peter 3:18).

"For there is one God and one mediator between God and men, the man Christ Jesus" (I Timothy 2:5).

"For God so loved the world that he gave his one and only Son, that whoever believes in him shall not perish but have eternal life" (John 3:16).

"Salvation is found in no one else, for there is no other name under heaven given to men by which we must be saved" (Acts 4:12).

3. Receive Christ by faith and accept the gift God has provided in His Son.

"Jesus answered, 'I am the way and the truth and the life. No one comes to the Father except through me'" (John 14:6).

"Yet to all who received him, to those who believed in his name, he gave the right to become children of God—" (John 1:12).

"Here I am! I stand at the door and knock. If anyone hears my voice and opens the door, I will come in..." (Revelation 3:20).

"...God has given us eternal life, and this life is in his Son. He who has the Son has life; he who does not have the Son of God does not have life" (I John 5:11-12).

4. Commit your whole life to the Lord Jesus Christ, and follow Him and serve Him without reserve.

"Whoever believes in the Son has eternal life, but whoever rejects the Son will not see life, for God's wrath remains on him" (John 3:36).

"...If anyone would come after me, he must deny himself and take up his cross and follow me" (Matthew 16:24).

"Anyone who loves his father or mother more than me is not worthy of me; anyone who loves his son or daughter more than me is not worthy of me; and anyone who does not take his cross and follow me is not worthy of me" (Matthew 10:37-38).

"'I tell you the truth,' Jesus said to them, 'No one who has left home or wife or brothers or parents or children for the sake of the kingdom of God will fail to receive many

times as much in this age and, in the age to come, eternal life'" (Luke 18:29-30).

5. Be prepared to confess Christ and to tell others that you belong to Him.

"...If you confess with your mouth, 'Jesus is Lord,' and believe in your heart that God raised him from the dead, you will be saved. For it is with your heart that you believe and are justified, and it is with your mouth that you confess and are saved" (Romans 10:9-10).

"Whoever acknowledges me before men, I will also acknowledge him before my Father in heaven. But whoever disowns me before men, I will disown him before my Father in heaven" (Matthew 10:32-33).

"If anyone is ashamed of me and my words, the Son of Man will be ashamed of him when he comes in his glory and in the glory of the Father and of the holy angels" (Luke 9:26).

6. Acknowledge that the Lord Jesus not only died upon the cross to give you eternal life, but that He rose again from the dead to live His life in you and through you.

"...Christ in you, the hope of glory" (Colossians 1:27).

"I have been crucified with Christ and I no longer live, but Christ lives in me. The life I live in the body, I live by faith in the Son of God, who loved me and gave himself for me" (Galatians 2:20).

- Your prayer of committal of your life to the Lord Jesus Christ:

Lord Jesus, I know that I am a sinner. I turn away from my sin in repentance, and ask You to forgive me. I believe You died on the cross for my sin, and I thank You with all my heart. I now invite You to come into my heart and life. By faith, I receive You as my Savior, and make You my Lord and Master. I place my whole life in Your hands without reserve. Thank You that You not only died to give me the gift of eternal life, but that You rose again to live Your life in me and through me. I am prepared to acknowledge You as my Lord before others, and in constant dependence upon the Holy Spirit, live for You in obedience to Your promptings. Thank You that according to Your Word, You have come in and made me Your child. Thank You that You have cleansed and forgiven me for my sin, and have given me eternal life.

Essentials for Progress as a Christian

1. Daily prayer, as well as daily reading of God's Word, is absolutely essential for you to grow spiritually strong.

You could start by reading the Gospel of John and the Psalms. Ask God, the Holy Spirit, to give you understanding, and then thank Him that He will.

"And without faith it is impossible to please God, because anyone who comes to him must believe that he exists and that he rewards those who earnestly seek him" (Hebrews 11:6).

Underline a verse when God speaks to you from it. The Bible is your guide and map.

"Your word is a lamp to my feet and a light for my path" (Psalm 119:105).

Do not confine prayers to "asking," but include thanksgiving and praise.

"...With thanksgiving, present your requests to God" (Philippians 4:6).

"Praise him for his acts of power; praise him for his surpassing greatness" (Psalm 150:2).

2. Seek God's guidance in all things, and expect Him to give it.

"I will instruct you and teach you in the way you should go; I will counsel you and watch over you" (Psalm 32:8).

He has promised to speak to us.

Some of the Ways of God in Healing

"My sheep hear my voice, and I know them, and they follow me" (John 10:27 RSV).

3. Meet regularly with other vital Christians in the church fellowship to which God leads you.

"They devoted themselves to the apostles' teaching and to the fellowship, to the breaking of bread and to prayer" (Acts 2:42).

"Let us not give up meeting together, as some are in the habit of doing, but let us encourage one another—and all the more as you see the Day approaching" (Hebrews 10:25).

4. An important method of public witness is to experience believer's baptism.

"As they traveled along the road, they came to some water and the eunuch said, 'Look, here is water. Why shouldn't I be baptized?'" (Acts 8:36).

By baptism, we make an open confession of our faith in the Lord Jesus Christ in the way in which He commanded us.

"Therefore go and make disciples of all nations, baptizing them in the name of the Father and of the Son and of the Holy Spirit" (Matthew 28:19).

5. Seek opportunities to lead others to Christ.

"...He who wins souls is wise" (Proverbs 11:30).

"'Come, follow Me,' Jesus said, 'and I will make you fishers of men'" (Matthew 4:19).

6. Remember that your enemy, the devil and his demons, will attack you in many ways, trying to make you sin.

James 4:7 says, *"Submit yourselves, then, to God. Resist the devil, and he will flee from you."* Say "It is written: '...Greater is he [the Lord Jesus Christ] that *is in [me] than he [the devil] that is in the world'"* (I John 4:4 KJV).

7. Should you fall into sin, do not be discouraged, but in repentance, confess all to the Lord.

"...Everyone who confesses the name of the Lord must turn away from wickedness" (II Timothy 2:19).

8. *"...Be filled with the Spirit"* (Ephesians 5:18).

God the Holy Spirit is a person who wants to completely control your life, so that the Lord Jesus Christ may be made real to you, and then through you to others.

Without His control, you will be a powerless, ineffective Christian.

a) Surrender your will totally to God.

"...the Holy Spirit, whom God has given to those who obey him" (Acts 5:32).

b) Be thorough in confession and repentance of all known sin.

"He who conceals his sins does not prosper, but whoever confesses and renounces them finds mercy" (Proverbs 28:13).

c) Ask God to fill you with His Spirit.

"If you then, though you are evil, know how to give good gifts to your children, how much more will your Father in heaven give the Holy Spirit to those who ask him!"
(Luke 11:13)

d) Believe that He will, and thank Him for doing so.

"...Everything that does not come from faith is sin" (Romans 14:23).

Some of the Ways of God in Healing

Allow the Holy Spirit to manifest Himself in whatever way He chooses, by being obedient to His promptings.

These conditions need to be fulfilled constantly in order to maintain the Spirit-filled life.

OTHER LIFE-CHANGING BOOKS
BY JOY DAWSON

- *Intimate Friendship with God*, 0-8007-9084-7 ($6.95) In the fascinating adventure of pursuing intimate friendship with the only One who can totally fulfill us, Joy makes it clear that the price is high, but that the privileges and rewards are higher. Read it. You'll want to take the journey, and be ruined for the ordinary.

- *How to Pray for Someone Near You Who is Away from God*, 0-96155-347-2 ($1.95) Been praying for unconverted loved ones and friends for years? Joy takes penetrating probes into some aspects of prayer, which when applied, bring results – in us, and accelerate the answers to our prayers for others.

- *The Character of the One Who Says "Go"*, 0-92754-508-X ($2.95) "...into all the world and preach the good news..."

Afraid God might call you to Africa?... or wherever? As Joy describes facets of God's intriguing character, we find that: *1)* Satan's lies about what God is really like are exposed. *2)* We discover that we do ourselves the greatest favor by being available and obedient to the most exciting Being in the universe.

LIFE-CHANGING BOOKS AND CASSETTES FROM YOUTH WITH A MISSION

YWAM Books:

- *Is That Really You God?*, by Loren Cunningham ($6.95) The exciting history of Youth With A Mission. In this book you see how an ordinary man who was committed to hearing God and obeying Him, became the founder of an extraordinary mission organization. An adventure in hearing and obeying the voice of God.

- *Anchor in the Storm*, by Helen Applegate ($6.95) The gripping true story of how Helen and her husband Ben, former captain of the mercy ship, M/V Anastasis, persevered through insurmountable odds to hold on to their dream to serve God on the high seas.

- *Before You Hit the Wall*, by Danny Lehmann ($6.95) The Christian life is likened unto the training of the marathon runner. This practical book shows how the disciplined life is not only attainable but enjoyable. It will equip you to "run" your spiritual race victoriously.

- *Daring to Live on the Edge: The Adventure of Faith and Finances*, by Loren Cunningham ($7.95) A compelling, fresh look at the subject of faith and finances by one of America's premier missions statesmen. This book will challenge and equip all who want to obey God's call, but who wonder where the money will come from.

- *The Father Heart of God*, by Floyd McClung ($5.95) Floyd, Executive Director of YWAM, shares how to know God as a loving, caring Father and a healer of our hurts.

- *Intimate Friendship with God*, by Joy Dawson ($6.95) Keys to knowing, obeying, and loving God by this dynamic teacher.

- *Leadership for the 21st Century*, by Ron Boehme ($7.95) At the close of the century, how will you lead? A great book with the goal of changing the nations through the power of serving.

- *Learning to Love People You Don't Like*, by Floyd McClung ($6.95) Knowing that biblical unity is not always easy, this book shares keys for loving others, even when it is hard.

- *Living on the Devil's Doorstep*, by Floyd McClung ($8.95) Join Floyd and his wife, Sally, in urban missions with YWAM, as they live first in a hippie hotel in Kabul, Afghanistan, and then next door to prostitutes, pimps, drug dealers, and homosexuals in Amsterdam, Holland.

- *Personal Prayer Diary-Daily Planner* ($11.95) What you get: quiet time journal, daily agenda, weekly goals, systematic Scripture readings, unreached people groups to pray for, prayer journal, concise teaching section, 9 pages of maps, and much more.

- *Some of the Ways of God in Healing*, by Joy Dawson ($6.95) All-out integrity from the author in the probing of scripture on the subject. Joy is ruthless in her pursuit of truth.

- *Spiritual Warfare for Every Christian*, by Dean Sherman ($6.95) Spiritual Warfare requires Spirit-controlled thinking and attitudes. Dean delivers a no-nonsense, practical approach to living in victory.

- *Streetwise*, by John Goodfellow ($6.95) John's pursuit of freedom only brought him deeper into the web of bondage. A compelling story of God's pursuit of one man and how He gave him true freedom.

- *Taking Our Cities for God*, by John Dawson (7.95) New bestseller on how to break spiritual strongholds. John Dawson gives you the strategies and tactics for taking your cities.

- *Target Earth*, by University of the Nations/Global Mapping Int'l ($27.95) This 170 page, full color atlas is filled with facts, maps, and articles by some fifty contributors.

- *Walls of My Heart*, by Dr. Bruce Thompson ($8.95) Dr. Bruce's popular teaching, now in book form, deals with the wounds and hurts that we all receive, and how to receive biblical healing.

- *We Cannot but Tell*, by Ross Tooley ($6.95) How to evangelize with love and compassion. Great for group studies as well as personal growth. Learn to reach out from your heart.

- *Winning, God's Way*, by Loren Cunningham ($6.95) Winning comes through laying down your life. This book gives the reader a look at the Cunningham's personal struggles and victories. A classic teaching of YWAM.

YWAM Tape Albums:

- "Let's Turn the World Around," by Loren Cunningham. An album of 6 audio cassettes ($24.95) Loren Cunningham founder of Youth With A Mission lays the basis for effectively changing the world with the Gospel.

- "Relationships," by Dean Sherman. An album of 6 audio cassettes ($24.95) Dean challenges us to live and walk in right relationships.

- "Spiritual Warfare," by Dean Sherman. An album of 12 audio cassettes ($39.95) Dean explores the many dynamics and strategies of spiritual warfare.

For a complete catalog of books and cassettes, write to the address below. To order any of the above listed books, write the title and quantity desired and send with the amount in US dollars.

FREE shipping at book rate with your order from this book.

Youth With A Mission Books
P.O. Box 55787
Seattle, WA 98155 USA
Tel. (206) 771-1153